# Let's Talk!

# Italian

SPARK PUBLISHING

SPARKNOTES is a registered trademark of SparkNotes LLC

Spark Publishing
A Division of Barnes & Noble Publishing
120 Fifth Avenue
New York, NY 10011
www.sparknotes.com

Please submit all comments and questions or report errors to
www.sparknotes.com/errors.

Printed and bound in the United States.

Library of Congress Cataloging-in-Publication Data

Let's Talk Italian.
    p. cm.
  ISBN-10: 1-4114-0444-0
  ISBN-13: 978-1-4114-0444-1
  1. Italian language—Conversation and phrase books—English.
  2. Italian language—Textbooks for foreign speakers—English.
PC1121.L48 2006
458.3'421—dc22

                                        2005026100

# Contents

# Starting from *Buongiorno*

## Greetings

**Good morning.**
Buongiorno.
*bwon-JOR-no.*

**Good afternoon.**
Buon pomeriggio.
*bwon po-me-REE-jo.*

**Good evening.**
Buonasera.
*bwo-na-SE-ra.*

**Hello / hi / hey.**
Ciao.
*chow.*

**What's up?**
Che mi racconti?
*ke mee ra-KON-tee?*

**Nothing much.**
Niente di speciale.
*NYEN-te dee spe-CHA-le.*

**How are you? / How's it going?**
Come stai? / Come va?
*ko-me stai? / ko-me va?*

## I'm ...
Sto ...
*sto ...*

### great.
benissimo.
*ben-EE-see-mo.*

### well / fine.
bene.
*BE-ne.*

### okay.
abbastanza bene.
*a-ba-STAN-za BE-ne.*

### not so great.
non benissimo.
*non ben-EE-see-mo.*

### very tired.
molto stanco/a.
*MOL-to STAN-ko.*

### broke—can I borrow some money?
squattrinato—mi presti dei soldi?
*skwa-tri-NA-to—mee PRE-stee de-ee SOL-dee?*

## How is your family?
Come sta la tua famiglia?
*ko-me sta la too-a fa-MEE-lyee-a?*

## How are your wife / husband and kids?
Come stanno tua moglie / tuo marito e i tuoi figli?
*ko-me STA-no too-a MO-lyee-e / too-o ma-REE-to
eh ee twoy FI-lyee?*

**Great, thanks. And you?**
Benissimo, grazie. E tu?
*ben-EE-see-mo, GRA-tzee-eh. eh too?*

# Goodbyes

**Goodbye.**
Arrivederci.
*a-ree-ve-DER-chee.*

**Bye.**
Ciao.
*chow.*

**So long. / Take care.**
Arrivederci. / Stammi bene.
*a-ree-ve-DER-chee. / STA-mee BE-ne.*

**See you soon.**
A presto.
*a PRE-sto.*

**See you later.**
A più tardi.
*a pyoo TAR-dee.*

**See you in the morning.**
A domattina.
*a do-ma-TEE-na.*

**Have ...**
Ti auguro ...
*tee ow-GOO-ro ...*

> **a nice day.**
> buona giornata.
> *BWO-na jor-NA-ta.*

### a great time.
buon divertimento.
*bwon dee-ver-tee-MEN-to.*

### a nice life.
una buona vita.
*oo-na BWO-na VEE-ta.*

~~~~~~~~~~~~~~~~~~~~

### Good night.
Buonanotte.
*bwo-na-NO-te.*

### Sleep well.
Dormi bene.
*DOR-mee BE-ne.*

### Sweet dreams.
Sogni d'oro.
*SO-nyee DO-ro.*

# Introductions

### What's your name?
Come ti chiami?
*ko-me tee KYA-mee?*

### My name is _____.
Mi chiamo _____.
*mee KYA-mo _____.*

### My friends call me _____.
I miei amici mi chiamano _____.
*ee myay a-MEE-chee mee KYA-ma-no _____.*

### Pleased to meet you.
Piacere (di conoscerti).
*pya-CHE-re (dee co-no-SHER-tee).*

**I've heard so much about you.**
Ho sentito tanto parlare di te.
*o sen-TEE-to TAN-to par-LA-re dee te.*

**It was nice to meet you.**
È stato un piacere (conoscerti).
*eh STA-to oon pya-CHE-re (co-no-SHER-tee).*

**I love your shoes.**
Che belle scarpe.
*ke BE-le SCAR-pe.*

**I'd like you to meet _____.**
Vorrei presentarti _____.
*vo-RE pre-zen-TAR-tee _____.*

**He / she's my friend.**
È un mio amico / una mia amica.
*eh oon mee-o a-MEE-ko / oo-na mee-a a-MEE-ka.*

**He / she's from _____.**
È di _____.
*eh dee _____.*

**He / she's a friend of _____'s.**
È un amico / un'amica di _____.
*e oon a-MEE-ko / oo-na-MEE-ka dee _____.*

**He / she's in town for_____ days.**
Si ferma qui _____ giorni.
*si FER-ma kwee _____ JOR-nee.*

**Do you speak English?**
Parli inglese?
*PAR-lee een-GLE-ze?*

**Your English is great!**
Parli benissimo l'inglese!
*PAR-lee be-NEE-see-mo leen-GLE-ze!*

**I speak only a little Italian.**
Parlo solo un po' d'italiano.
*PAR-lo SO-lo oon po dee-tal-YA-no.*

# Getting Help

**Can you help me, please?**
Puoi aiutarmi, per favore?
*pwoy ay-oo-TAR-mee, per fa-VO-re?*

**Can you do me a favor?**
Mi fai un favore?
*mee fai oon fa-VO-re?*

**Can you spare some change?**
Hai qualche spicciolo?
*ai KWAL-ke SPEE-cho-lo?*

**Would you mind ...**
Ti spiacerebbe ...
*tee spya-che-RE-be ...*

> **watching my bag?**
> dare un'occhiata alla mia borsa?
> *DA-re oo-no-KYA-ta a-la mee-a BOR-sa?*

> **saving my seat?**
> tenermi il posto?
> *te-NER-mee eel POS-to?*

> **spreading this suntan lotion on my back?**
> spalmarmi la crema solare sulla schiena?
> *spal-MAR-mee la KRE-ma so-LA-re SOO-la SKYE-na?*

# Pleasantries

**Thank you.**
Grazie.
*GRA-tzee-e.*

**I really appreciate it.**
Lo apprezzo molto.
*lo a-PRE-tzo MOL-to.*

**You're welcome.**
Prego.
*PRE-go.*

**Don't mention it.**
Figurati.
*fee-goo-RA-tee.*

**Excuse me.**
Scusami.
*SKOO-za-mee.*

**Sorry.**
Scusa.
*SKOO-za.*

**Can you ever forgive me?**
Potrai mai perdonarmi?
*po-TRAI mai per-do-NAR-mee?*

## Asking

| who? | chi? | *kee?* |
|---|---|---|
| **what?** | cosa? | *KO-za?* |
| **when?** | quando? | *KWAN-do?* |
| **where?** | dove? | *DO-ve?* |
| **why?** | perché? | *per-KE?* |
| **which?** | quale? | *KWA-le?* |
| **how?** | come? | *KO-me?* |
| **how much?** | quanto? | *KWAN-to?* |
| **how many?** | quanti? | *KWAN-ti?* |

# Answering

| | | |
|---|---|---|
| **yes** | sì | *see* |
| **no** | no | *no* |
| **maybe** | forse | *FOR-se* |

# Numbers

| 0 | zero | *TZE-ro* |
|---|---|---|
| 1 | uno | *OO-no* |
| 2 | due | *DOO-e* |
| 3 | tre | *tre* |
| 4 | quattro | *KWA-tro* |
| 5 | cinque | *CHEEN-kwe* |
| 6 | sei | *se* |
| 7 | sette | *SE-te* |
| 8 | otto | *O-to* |
| 9 | nove | *NO-ve* |
| 10 | dieci | *dee-E-chee* |
| 11 | undici | *OON-dee-chee* |
| 12 | dodici | *DO-dee-chee* |
| 13 | tredici | *TRE-dee-chee* |
| 14 | quattordici | *kwa-TOR-dee-chee* |
| 15 | quindici | *KWEEN-dee-chee* |
| 16 | sedici | *SE-dee-chee* |
| 17 | diciassette | *dee-cha-SE-te* |

STARTING FROM BUONGIORNO

| 18 | diciotto | *dee-CHO-to* |
|---|---|---|
| 19 | diciannove | *dee-cha-NO-ve* |
| 20 | venti | *VEN-tee* |
| 21 | ventuno | *ven-TOO-no* |
| 22 | ventidue | *ven-tee-DOO-e* |
| 30 | trenta | *TREN-ta* |
| 40 | quaranta | *kwa-RAN-ta* |
| 50 | cinquanta | *cheen-KWAN-ta* |
| 60 | sessanta | *se-SAN-ta* |
| 70 | settanta | *se-TAN-ta* |
| 80 | ottanta | *o-TAN-ta* |
| 90 | novanta | *no-VAN-ta* |
| 100 | cento | *CHEN-to* |
| 200 | duecento | *DOO-e-chen-to* |
| 500 | cinquecento | *CHEEN-kwe-chen-to* |
| 1,000 | mille | *MEE-le* |
| 100,000 | centomila | *chen-to-MEE-la* |
| 1,000,000 | un milione | *oon mee-LYO-ne* |

| **first** | primo/a | *PREE-mo* |
|---|---|---|
| **second** | secondo/a | *se-CON-do* |
| **third** | terzo/a | *TER-tzo* |
| **fourth** | quarto/a | *KWAR-to* |
| **fifth** | quinto/a | *KWEEN-to* |
| **sixth** | sesto/a | *SES-to* |
| **seventh** | settimo/a | *SE-tee-mo* |
| **eighth** | ottavo/a | *o-TAV-o* |

| ninth | nono/a | *NO-no* |
| **tenth** | decimo/a | *DE-chee-mo* |
| **one-half / a half** | mezzo/a | *ME-tzo* |
| **one-third / a third** | un terzo | *oon TER-tzo* |
| **one-fourth / a quarter** | un quarto | *oon KWAR-to* |

**How old are you?**
Quanti anni hai?
*KWAN-tee A-nee ai?*

**I'm [23] years old.**
Ho [23] anni.
*o [ven-tee-TRE] A-nee.*

**How much does this cost?**
Quanto costa?
*KWAN-to KO-sta?*

**It costs [27] euros.**
Costa [27] euro.
*KO-sta [ven-tee-SE-te] YOO-ro.*

# Colors

| **white** | bianco | *BYAN-ko* |
| **pink** | rosa | *RO-za* |
| **purple** | viola | *VYO-la* |
| **red** | rosso | *RO-so* |
| **orange** | arancione | *a-ran-CHO-ne* |
| **yellow** | giallo | *JA-lo* |

| green | verde | *VER-de* |
| blue | blu | *bloo* |
| brown | marrone | *ma-RO-ne* |
| gray | grigio | *GREE-jo* |
| black | nero | *NE-ro* |

# Months and Seasons

| January | gennaio | *je-NAI-o* |
| February | febbraio | *fe-BRAI-o* |
| March | marzo | *MAR-tzo* |
| April | aprile | *a-PREE-le* |
| May | maggio | *MA-jo* |
| June | giugno | *JOO-nyo* |
| July | luglio | *LOO-lyo* |
| August | agosto | *a-GO-sto* |
| September | settembre | *se-TEM-bre* |
| October | ottobre | *o-TO-bre* |
| November | novembre | *no-VEM-bre* |
| December | dicembre | *di-CHEM-bre* |

| spring | primavera | *pree-MA-ve-ra* |
| summer | estate | *e-STA-te* |
| fall / autumn | autunno | *ow-TOO-no* |
| winter | inverno | *een-VER-no* |

**[two] months ago**
[due] mesi fa
*[doo-e] ME-zee fa*

**last month**
il mese scorso
*eel ME-ze SKOR-so*

**this month**
questo mese
*KWE-sto ME-ze*

**next month**
il mese prossimo
*eel ME-ze PRO-see-mo*

**in [two] months**
fra [due] mesi
*fra [DOO-e] ME-zee*

**[two] years ago**
[due] anni fa
*[DOO-e] A-nee fa*

**last year**
l'anno scorso
*LA-no SKOR-so*

**this year**
quest'anno
*kwes-TA-no*

**next year**
l'anno prossimo
*LA-no PRO-see-mo*

**in [two] years**
fra [due] anni
*fra [DOO-e] A-nee*

# Days and Weeks

| **Monday** | lunedì | *loo-ne-DEE* |
|---|---|---|
| **Tuesday** | martedì | *mar-te-DEE* |
| **Wednesday** | mercoledì | *mer-co-le-DEE* |
| **Thursday** | giovedì | *jo-ve-DEE* |
| **Friday** | venerdì | *ve-ner-DEE* |
| **Saturday** | sabato | *SA-ba-to* |
| **Sunday** | domenica | *do-ME-nee-ka* |

**[three] days ago**
[tre] giorni fa
*[tre] JOR-nee fa*

**the day before yesterday**
l'altroieri
*lal-tro-YE-ree*

**yesterday**
ieri
*YE-ree*

**today**
oggi
*O-jee*

**tomorrow**
domani
*do-MA-nee*

**the day after tomorrow**
dopodomani
*do-po-do-MA-nee*

**in [three] days**
fra [tre] giorni
*fra [tre] JOR-nee*

**weekend**
fine settimana
*FEE-ne se-tee-MA-na*

**last [Monday]**
[lunedì] scorso
*[loo-ne-DEE] SKOR-so*

**this [Monday]**
questo [lunedì]
*KWE-sto [loo-ne-DEE]*

**next [Monday]**
[lunedì] prossimo
*[loo-ne-DEE] PRO-see-mo*

**What day of the week is it?**
Che giorno è?
*ke JOR-no eh?*

**What's today's date?**
Quanti ne abbiamo oggi?
*KWAN-tee ne ab-YA-mo O-jee?*

**It's [September 16th].**
È il [16 settembre].
*eh eel [SE-dee-chee se-TEM-bre].*

**Today is the [16th].**
Oggi è il [16].
*O-jee eh eel [SE-dee-chee].*

**[two] weeks ago**
[due] settimane fa
*[DOO-e] se-tee-MA-ne fa*

**last week**
la settimana scorsa
*la se-tee-MA-na SKOR-sa*

**this week**
questa settimana
*KWE-sta se-tee-MA-na*

**next week**
la settimana prossima
*la se-tee-MA-na PRO-see-ma*

**in [two] weeks**
fra [due] settimane
*fra [DOO-e] se-tee-MA-ne*

# Telling Time

**Excuse me, what time is it?**
Scusa, che ora è / che ore sono?
*SCOO-za, ke O-ra eh / ke O-re SO-no?*

**It's ...**
Sono le ...
*SO-no le ...*

### 9:00 [in the morning].
nove [di mattina].
*NO-ve [dee ma-TEE-na].*

### 3:00 [in the afternoon].
tre [del pomeriggio].
*TRE [del po-me-REE-jo].*

### 7:00 [in the evening].
sette [di sera].
*SE-te [dee SE-ra].*

### 10:00 [at night].
dieci [di sera].
*dee-E-chee [dee SE-ra].*

### 2:00 [in the morning].
due [del mattino].
*DOO-e [del ma-TEE-no].*

**4:00.**
quattro.
*KWA-tro.*

**4:10.**
quattro e dieci.
*KWA-tro eh dee-E-chee.*

**4:15 (quarter past 4).**
quattro e un quarto.
*KWA-tro eh oon KWAR-to.*

**4:20.**
quattro e venti.
*KWA-tro eh VEN-tee.*

**4:30 (half past 4).**
quattro e mezza.
*KWA-tro eh ME-tza.*

**4:45 (quarter to 5).**
cinque meno un quarto.
*CHEEN-kwe ME-no oon KWAR-to.*

**4:50 (ten to 5).**
cinque meno dieci.
*CHEEN-kwe ME-no dee-E-chee.*

**It's ...**
È ...
*eh ...*

**noon.**
mezzogiorno.
*me-tzo-JOR-no.*

**midnight.**
mezzanotte.
*me-tza-NO-te.*

**morning.**
mattina.
*ma-TEE-na.*

**day.**
giorno.
*JOR-no.*

**afternoon.**
pomeriggio.
*po-me-REE-jo.*

**evening.**
sera.
*SE-ra.*

**night.**
notte.
*NO-te.*

---

**[two] nights ago**
[due] sere fa
*[DOO-e] SE-re fa*

**last night**
ieri sera
*YE-ree SE-ra*

**tonight**
stasera
*sta-SE-ra*

**tomorrow night**
domani sera
*do-MA-nee SE-ra*

**the morning after**
la mattina dopo
*la ma-TEE-na DO-po*

### How long will it take?
Quanto ci vorrà?
*KWAN-to chee vo-RA?*

#### An hour.
Un'ora.
*oo-NO-ra.*

#### [Two] hours.
[Due] ore.
*[DOO-e] O-re.*

#### Half an hour.
Mezz'ora.
*me-TZO-ra.*

#### [Ten] minutes.
[Dieci] minuti.
*[dee-E-chee] mee-NOO-tee.*

### before
prima
*PREE-ma*

### after
dopo
*DO-po*

### during
durante
*doo-RAN-te*

### [two] hours ago
[due] ore fa
*[DOO-e] O-re fa*

### in [two] hours
fra [due] ore
*fra [DOO-e] O-re*

**[two] hours later**
[due] ore dopo
*[DOO-e]  O-re  DO-po*

**[two] hours earlier**
[due] ore prima
*[DOO-e]  O-re  PREE-ma*

~~~~~~~~~~~~~~~~

**See you ...**
Ci vediamo ...
*chee  ve-DYA-mo  ...*

> **tomorrow morning.**
> domattina.
> *do-ma-TEE-na.*

> **[Tuesday] night.**
> [martedì] sera.
> *mar-te-DEE  SE-ra.*

~~~~~~~~~~~~~~~~

**every day**
ogni giorno
*O-nyee  JOR-no*

**forever**
per sempre
*per  SEM-pre*

**always**
sempre
*SEM-pre*

**sometimes**
qualche volta
*KWAL-ke  VOL-ta*

**never**
mai
*MAI*

# Getting There

**2**

## Tickets

**I'd like a ... ticket**
Vorrei un biglietto ...
*vo-RE oon bee-LYET-o ...*

> **one-way**
> di sola andata
> *dee SO-la an-DA-ta*
>
> **round-trip**
> di andata e ritorno
> *dee an-DA-ta eh ree-TOR-no*
>
> **student**
> da studente
> *da stoo-DEN-te*
>
> **cheap**
> conveniente
> *kon-ven-YEN-te*
>
> **economy / coach class**
> in economy
> *een e-KO-no-mee*
>
> **business class**
> in business class
> *een BEEZ-nes klas*
>
> **first class**
> di prima classe
> *dee PREE-ma KLA-se*

### ticket counter
biglietteria
*bee-lyet-e-REE-a*

### discount
sconto
*SCON-to*

### I'd like a one-way ticket to [Milan], please.
Vorrei un biglietto di sola andata per [Milano],
per favore.
*vo-RE oon bee-LYET-o dee SO-la an-DA-ta per [mee-LA-no],
per fa-VO-re.*

### I need to ...
Devo ...
*DE-vo ...*

#### change my ticket.
cambiare il mio biglietto.
*kam-BYA-re eel mee-o bee-LYET-o.*

#### return my ticket.
restituire il mio biglietto.
*re-stee-TWEE-re eel mee-o bee-LYET-o.*

### I lost my ticket.
Ho perso il mio biglietto.
*o PER-so eel mee-o bee-LYET-o.*

### I demand a refund.
Chiedo un rimborso.
*KYE-do oon reem-BOR-so.*

# Making Reservations

**I'm staying ...**
Sto ...
*sto ...*

### in a hotel.
in un albergo.
*een oon al-BER-go.*

### at an inn.
in una pensione.
*een oo-na pen-SYO-ne.*

### at a bed-and-breakfast.
in un bed and breakfast.
*een oon bed and BREK-fast.*

### at a hostel.
in un ostello.
*een oon o-STE-lo.*

### at a campsite.
in un campeggio.
*een oon kam-PE-jo.*

### by the beach.
vicino alla spiaggia.
*vee-CHEE-no a-la SPYA-ja.*

### with a friend.
da un amico.
*da oon a-MEE-ko.*

### with you!
da te!
*da te!*

### I'd like to make a reservation ...
Vorrei fare una prenotazione ...
*vo-RE FA-re oo-na pre-no-ta-TZYO-ne ...*

### for one night.
per una notte.
*per oo-na NO-te.*

### for two nights.
per due notti.
*per DOO-e NO-tee.*

### for three nights.
per tre notti.
*per tre NO-tee.*

### for a week.
per una settimana.
*per oo-na se-tee-MA-na.*

### for one person.
per una persona.
*per oo-na per-SO-na.*

### for two people.
per due persone.
*per DOO-e per-SO-ne.*

### for two girls.
per due ragazze.
*per DOO-e ra-GA-tze.*

### for two guys.
per due ragazzi.
*per DOO-e ra-GA-tzee.*

### for a couple.
per una coppia.
*per oo-na KO-pee-a.*

## Do you take credit cards?
Prendete la carta di credito?
*pren-DE-te la KAR-ta dee KRE-dee-to?*

---

## How much is ...
Quant'è / Quanto costa ...
*kwan-TE / KWAN-to KO-sta ...*

### a room ...
una stanza ...
*oo-na STAN-za ...*

### a single room ...
una (stanza) singola ...
*oo-na (STAN-za) SEEN-go-la ...*

### a double room ...
una (stanza) doppia ...
*oo-na (STAN-za) DO-pya ...*

#### with a shower?
con la doccia?
*kon la DO-cha?*

#### with a bathtub?
con la vasca da bagno?
*kon la VA-sca da BA-nyo?*

#### with a sink?
con il lavandino?
*kon eel la-van-DEE-no?*

#### with a toilet?
con i servizi?
*kon ee ser-VEE-tzee?*

#### with a TV?
con la televisione?
*kon la te-le-vee-ZYO-ne?*

### with a refrigerator?
con il frigo?
*kon eel FREE-go?*

### with air-conditioning?
con l'aria condizionata?
*kon LAR-ya kon-dee-tzyo-NA-ta?*

### a private room
una (stanza) singola
*oo-na (STAN-za) SEEN-go-la*

### a shared room
una camerata
*oo-na ka-me-RA-ta*

### a bunk bed
un letto a castello
*oon LE-to a ka-STE-lo*

### an extra bed
un letto supplementare
*oon LE-to soo-ple-men-TA-re*

| **male** | maschio | *MA-skyo* |
|---|---|---|
| **female** | femmina | *fe-MEE-na* |
| **single-sex** | non misto/a | *non MEE-sto/a* |
| **co-ed** | misto/a | *MEE-sto/a* |

### Do you provide ...
Fornite ...
*for-NEE-te ...*

#### bedding?
lenzuola e coperte?
*len-ZWO-la e ko-PER-te?*

**sheets?**
lenzuola?
*len-ZWO-la?*

**towels?**
asciugamani?
*a-shoo-ga-MA-nee?*

**toiletries?**
accessori da toletta?
*a-che-SO-ree da to-LE-ta?*

**a mini-bar?**
il minibar?
*eel mi-ni-BAR?*

**Is there ...**
C'è ...
*che ...*

| | | |
|---|---|---|
| **a pool?** | la piscina? | *la pee-SHEE-na?* |
| **a gym?** | la palestra? | *la pa-LE-stra?* |
| **a kitchen?** | la cucina? | *la koo-CHEE-na?* |

**What time is ...**
A che ora è ...
*a ke O-ra e ...*

| | | |
|---|---|---|
| **check-in?** | il check-in? | *eel chek-een?* |
| **checkout?** | il checkout? | *eel chek-owt?* |

**Can I leave my luggage for the day?**
Posso lasciare qui il mio bagaglio per oggi?
*PO-so la-SHA-re kwee eel mee-o ba-GA-lyo per O-jee?*

### Do I need my own lock?
Devo prendermi un lucchetto?
*DE-vo pren-DER-mee oon loo-KE-to?*

---

### Please give me directions ...
Per favore, dimmi come arrivo ...
*per fa-VO-re, DEE-mee CO-me a-REE-vo ...*

#### from the airport.
dall'aeroporto.
*da-lai-ro-POR-to.*

#### from the train station.
dalla stazione (dei treni).
*DA-la sta-TZYO-ne (de-ee TRE-nee).*

#### from the bus station.
dalla stazione degli autobus.
*DA-la sta-TZYO-ne de-lyee ow-to-BOOS.*

# In Transit

### I'm traveling ...
Viaggio ...
*vee-A-jo ...*

#### by airplane.
in aereo.
*een AI-re-o.*

#### by train / rail.
in treno.
*een TRE-no.*

#### by subway.
in metro.
*een ME-tro.*

**by bus.**
in autobus.
*een ow-to-BOOS.*

**by car.**
in macchina / auto.
*een MA-kee-na / OW-to.*

**by taxi.**
in taxi.
*een TA-ksee.*

**by bicycle.**
in bici.
*een BEE-chee.*

**on horseback.**
a cavallo.
*a ka-VA-lo.*

**on foot.**
a piedi.
*a PYED-ee.*

**with friends.**
con degli amici.
*kon de-lyee a-MEE-chee.*

**with my parents.**
con i miei genitori.
*kon ee myay je-nee-TO-ree.*

**with my entourage.**
con il mio seguito.
*kon eel mee-o se-GWEE-to.*

**alone.**
da solo / da sola.
*da SO-lo / da SO-la.*

# Air Travel

**flight**
volo
*VO-lo*

**airport**
aeroporto
*ai-ro-POR-to*

**airline**
compagnia aerea
*kom-pa-NYEE-a AI-re-a*

**connection**
coincidenza
*ko-een-chee-DEN-za*

**layover**
tappa
*TA-pa*

**delay**
ritardo
*ree-TAR-do*

**ticket**
biglietto
*bee-LYET-o*

**pilot**
pilota
*pee-LO-ta*

**flight attendant**
hostess (f.) / steward (m.)
*O-stes / STOO-ard*

## Where is / are ...
Dov'è / Dove sono ...
*do-VE / DO-ve SO-no ...*

### check-in?
il check-in?
*eel chek-een?*

### departures?
le partenze?
*le par-TEN-tze?*

### arrivals?
gli arrivi?
*lyee a-REE-vee?*

### the gate?
il cancello d'imbarco / l'uscita / il gate?
*eel kan-CHE-lo deem-BAR-ko / loo-SHEE-ta /*
*eel geht?*

### baggage claim?
il ritiro bagagli?
*eel ree-TEE-ro ba-GA-lyee?*

### lost-and-found?
gli oggetti smarriti?
*lyee o-JE-tee zma-REE-tee?*

### the bar?
il bar?
*eel bar?*

## I'm on flight [101] to [Rome].
Sono sul volo [101] per [Roma].
*SO-no sool VO-lo [CHEN-to OO-no] per [RO-ma].*

## What time does the flight to [Naples] leave?
A che ora è il volo per [Napoli]?
*a ke O-ra eh eel VO-lo per [NA-po-lee]?*

### Which gate does it leave from?
Da che uscita parte?
*da ke oo-SHEE-ta PAR-te?*

### I need to check two bags.
Ho due borse.
*o DOO-e BOR-se.*

### I only have carry-on luggage.
Ho solo il bagaglio a mano.
*o SO-lo eel ba-GA-lyo a MA-no.*

### I need a boarding pass.
Mi serve una carta d'imbarco.
*mee SER-ve oo-na CAR-ta deem-BAR-co.*

### Is the flight ...
Il volo è ...
*eel VO-lo eh ...*

| | | |
|---|---|---|
| **on time?** | in orario? | *een o-RA-ryo?* |
| **early?** | in anticipo? | *een an-TEE-chee-po?* |
| **late?** | in ritardo? | *een ree-TAR-do?* |
| **delayed?** | ritardato? | *ree-tar-DA-to?* |
| **canceled?** | cancellato? | *kan-che-LA-to?* |

### I'm in ...
Sono in ...
*SO-no een ...*

#### first class.
prima classe.
*PREE-ma KLA-se.*

#### business class.
business class.
*BEES-nes klas.*

### economy / coach.
economy.
*e-KO-no-mee.*

### the bathroom.
bagno.
*BA-nyo.*

---

## I have a(n) ...
Ho un ...
*o oon ...*

### aisle seat.
posto corridoio.
*PO-sto ko-ree-DOY-o.*

### window seat.
posto finestrino.
*PO-sto fee-ne-STREE-no.*

---

## My luggage is ...
Il mio bagaglio è ...
*eel mee-o ba-GA-lyo e ...*

### missing.
smarrito.
*zma-REE-to.*

### damaged.
danneggiato.
*da-ne-JA-to.*

### really heavy.
molto pesante.
*MOL-to pe-ZAN-te.*

# Train Travel

**train**
treno
*TRE-no*

**tracks**
binari
*bee-NA-ree*

**baggage locker**
armadietto
*ar-ma-DYTE-o*

**compartment**
scompartimento
*skom-par-tee-MEN-to*

**dining car**
vagone ristorante
*va-GO-ne ree-sto-RAN-te*

**Where is the train station?**
Dov'è la stazione dei treni?
*do-VE la sta-TZYO-ne (de-ee TRE-nee)?*

**I'm on the [5:00] train to [Florence].**
Sono sul treno delle [5:00] per [Firenze].
*SO-no sool TRE-no de-le [CHEEN-kwe] per [fee-REN-ze].*

**What time does the train to [Turin] leave?**
A che ora parte il treno per [Torino]?
*a ke O-ra PAR-te eel TRE-no per [to-REE-no]?*

**Which platform does it leave from?**
Da che binario parte?
*da ke bee-NAR-ee-o PAR-te?*

## I'd like a ticket ...
Vorrei un posto ...
*vo-RE oon PO-sto ...*

### in the smoking section.
nello scompartimento fumatori.
*ne-lo skom-par-tee-MEN-to foo-ma-TO-ree.*

### in the nonsmoking section.
nello scompartimento non fumatori.
*ne-lo skom-par-tee-MEN-to non foo-ma-TO-ree.*

### on the overnight train.
sul treno notturno.
*sool TRE-no no-TOOR-no.*

### in the sleeping car.
in cuccetta.
*een koo-CHE-ta.*

## I need ...
Vorrei ...
*vo-RE ...*

### some sheets.
delle lenzuola.
*de-le len-ZWO-la.*

### a blanket.
una coperta.
*oo-na ko-PER-ta.*

### some pillows.
dei cuscini.
*de-ee koo-SHEE-nee.*

# Bus Travel

### Where is the bus station?
Dov'è la stazione degli autobus?
*do-VE la sta-TZYO-ne de-lyee ow-to-BOOS?*

### Do I need a reservation?
Devo prenotare?
*DE-vo pre-no-TA-re?*

### Can you turn up the heat, please?
Può aumentare il riscaldamento, per favore?
*pwo ow-men-TA-re eel ree-skal-da-MEN-to, per fa-VO-re?*

### Can you turn down the heat, please?
Può diminuire il riscaldamento, per favore?
*pwo dee-mee-noo-EE-re eel ree-skal-da-MEN-to, per fa-VO-re?*

### How much longer?
Quanto manca?
*KWAN-to MAN-ka?*

### Are we there yet?
Siamo arrivati?
*SYA-mo a-ree-VA-tee?*

# Passport and Customs

### passport
passaporto
*pa-sa-POR-to*

### visa
visto
*VEE-sto*

**ID**
carta d'identità
*KAR-ta dee-den-tee-TA*

**driver's license**
patente (di guida)
*pa-TEN-te (dee GWEE-da)*

**customs**
dogana
*do-GA-na*

**declaration form**
dichiarazione
*dee-kya-ra-TZYO-ne*

---

**I'm traveling ...**
Sono in viaggio ...
*SO-no een vee-A-jo ...*

> **on business.** d'affari. *da-FAR-ee.*

> **for pleasure.** di piacere. *dee pya-CHE-re.*

---

**I'm an [American] citizen.**
Sono un cittadino/a [americano/a].
*SO-no oon chee-ta-DEE-no [a-me-ree-KA-no].*

**I lost my passport.**
Ho perso il passaporto.
*o PER-so eel pa-sa-POR-to.*

---

**I plan to stay ...**
Ho intenzione di fermarmi ...
*o een-ten-TZYO-ne dee fer-MAR-mee ...*

> **for [three] days.**
> per [tre] giorni.
> *per [tre] JOR-nee.*

### for [one] month.
per [un] mese.
*per [oon] ME-ze.*

### forever.
per sempre.
*per SEM-pre.*

### until I find what I'm looking for.
finché non trovo quel che sto cercando.
*feen-KE non TRO-vo kwel ke sto cher-KAN-do.*

### until I clear my name.
finché non ristabilisco la mia reputazione.
*feen-KE non ree-sta-bee-LEE-sko la mee-a re-poo-ta-TZYO-ne.*

### I'm only passing through.
Sono solo di passaggio.
*SO-no SO-lo dee pa-SA-jo.*

### I have nothing to declare.
Non ho niente da dichiarare.
*non o NYEN-te da dee-kya-RA-re.*

# Countries and Nationalities

### England / English
Inghilterra / inglese
*een-gil-TE-ra / een-GLE-ze*

### France / French
Francia / francese
*FRAN-cha / fran-CHE-ze*

### Spain / Spanish
Spagna / spagnolo/a
*SPA-nya / spa-NYO-lo*

**Portugal / Portuguese**
Portogallo / portoghese
*por-to-GA-lo  /  por-to-GE-ze*

**Italy / Italian**
Italia / italiano/a
*ee-TAL-ya  /  ee-tal-YA-no*

**Greece / Greek**
Grecia / greco/a
*GRE-cha  /  GRE-ko*

**Germany / German**
Germania / tedesco/a
*jer-MAN-ya  /  te-DE-sko*

**Russia / Russian**
Russia / russo/a
*ROO-sya  /  ROO-so*

**United States / American**
Stati Uniti / americano/a
*STA-tee  oo-NEE-tee  /  a-me-ree-KA-no*

**Canada / Canadian**
Canada / canadese
*KA-na-da  /  ka-na-DE-ze*

**Mexico / Mexican**
Messico / messicano/a
*ME-see-ko  /  me-see-KA-no*

**Brazil / Brazilian**
Brasile / brasiliano/a
*bra-ZEE-le  /  bra-zeel-YA-no*

**Argentina / Argentine**
Argentina / argentino/a
*ar-jen-TEE-na  /  ar-jen-TEE-no*

**Morocco / Moroccan**
Marocco / marocchino/a
*ma-RO-ko  /  ma-ro-KEE-no*

**Egypt / Egyptian**
Egitto / egiziano/a
*e-JEE-to / e-jee-TZYA-no*

**Israel / Israeli**
Israele / israeliano/a
*ees-ra-E-le / ees-ra-e-LYA-no*

**China / Chinese**
Cina / cinese
*CHEE-na / chee-NE-ze*

**India / Indian**
India / indiano/a
*EEN-dya / een-DYA-no*

**Korea / Korean**
Corea / coreano/a
*ko-RE-a / ko-re-A-no*

**Japan / Japanese**
Giappone / giapponese
*ja-PO-ne / ja-po-NE-ze*

**Thailand / Thai**
Tailandia / tailandese
*tai-LAN-dya / tai-lan-DE-ze*

**Australia /Australian**
Australia / australiano/a
*ow-STRA-lya / ow-stra-LYA-no*

**New Zealand / Kiwi**
Nuova Zelanda / neozelandese
*NWO-va ze-LAN-da / ne-o-ze-lan-DE-ze*

# 3 Settling In

## Checking In

**reception**
reception
*re-SEP-shon*

**check-in**
check-in
*chek-een*

**checkout**
checkout
*chek-owt*

**deposit**
deposito
*de-PO-zee-to*

**key**
chiave
*KYA-ve*

**keycard**
chiave magnetica
*KYA-ve ma-NYET-ee-ka*

**Do I need a reservation?**
Devo prenotare?
*DE-vo pre-no-TA-re?*

### I'd like to check in.

Vorrei fare il check-in.
*vo-RE FA-re eel chek-een.*

### I have a reservation for tonight.

Ho una prenotazione per stasera.
*o oo-na pre-no-ta-TZYO-ne per sta-SE-ra.*

### Can I change my reservation?

Posso cambiare la mia prenotazione?
*PO-so kam-BYA-re la mee-a pre-no-ta-TZYO-ne?*

### I'd like to cancel my reservation.

Vorrei cancellare la mia prenotazione.
*vo-RE kan-che-LA-re la mee-a pre-no-ta-TZYO-ne.*

### Is there an elevator?

C'è l'ascensore?
*che la-shen-SO-re?*

### Can you help me with my luggage?

Può aiutarmi con i bagagli?
*pwo ay-oo-TAR-mee kon ee ba-GA-lyee?*

### Can I have an extra key?

Posso avere una chiave in più?
*PO-so a-VE-re oo-na KYA-ve een pyoo?*

### Here is your tip. Thanks.

Ecco la mancia. Grazie.
*E-co la MAN-cha. GRA-tzee-e.*

---

### My room ...

La mia stanza ...
*la mee-a STAN-za ...*

#### is too small.

è troppo piccola.
*eh TRO-po PEE-ko-la.*

### is too dirty.
è troppo sporca.
*eh TRO-po SPOR-ka.*

### is too hot.
è troppo calda.
*eh TRO-po KAL-da.*

### is too cold.
è troppo fredda.
*eh TRO-po FRE-da.*

### is just right.
va benissimo.
*va be-NEE-see-mo.*

### is perfect.
è perfetta.
*eh per-FE-ta.*

### is crawling with ants.
brulica di formiche.
*broo-LEE-ka dee for-MEE-ke.*

---

### I need new sheets.
Vorrei delle lenzuola pulite.
*vo-RE de-le len-ZWO-la poo-LEE-te.*

---

### The ... doesn't work.
... non funziona.
*... non foon-ZYO-na.*

#### light switch
L'interruttore (della luce)
*leen-te-roo-TO-re (de-la LOO-che)*

#### alarm clock
La sveglia
*la SVE-lya*

### TV
La televisione
*la te-le-vee-ZYO-ne*

### sink
Il lavandino
*eel la-van-DEE-no*

### shower
La doccia
*la DO-cha*

### refrigerator
Il frigo
*eel FREE-go*

### air conditioning
L'aria condizionata
*LAR-ya kon-dee-tzyo-NA-ta*

### heat
Il riscaldamento
*eel ree-skal-da-MEN-to*

## The toilet doesn't work.
I servizi non funzionano.
*ee ser-VEE-tzee non foon-ZYO-na-no.*

## What is the phone number here?
Qual è il vostro numero di telefono?
*kwal e eel VO-stro NOO-me-ro dee te-LE-fo-no?*

## Are there any messages for me?
Ci sono messaggi per me?
*chee SO-no me-SA-jee per me?*

## I'm in room [212].
Sono nella stanza [212].
*so-no ne-la STAN-za [doo-e-CHEN-to DO-dee-chee].*

### I lost the key to my room.
Ho perso la chiave della mia stanza.
*o PER-so la KYA-ve de-la mee-a STAN-za.*

### What time is breakfast?
A che ora è la colazione?
*a ke O-ra e la ko-la-TZYO-ne?*

### Is there someone here all night?
C'è qualcuno qui di notte?
*che kwal-KOO-no kwee dee NO-te?*

### How late can I stay out?
Fino a che ora posso star fuori?
*FEE-no a ke O-ra PO-so star FWO-ree?*

### I need a wake-up call.
Vorrei essere svegliato.
*vo-RE E-ser-e sve-LYA-to.*

### Let me in!
Lasciami entrare!
*LA-sha-mee en-TRA-re!*

## Relief!

### toilet
bagno / servizi
*BA-nyo / ser-VEE-tzee*

### sink
lavandino
*la-van-DEE-no*

### toilet paper
carta igienica
*KAR-ta ee-jee-E-nee-ka*

### Where's ...
Dov'è ...
*do-VE ...*

#### the bathroom?
il bagno?
*eel BA-nyo?*

#### the ladies' room?
il bagno delle donne?
*eel BA-nyo de-le DO-ne?*

#### the men's room?
il bagno degli uomini?
*eel BA-nyo de-lyee WO-mee-nee?*

### It's not working.
Non funziona.
*non foon-ZYO-na.*

### It won't flush.
Lo sciacquone non funziona.
*lo sha-KWO-ne non foon-ZYO-na.*

### It's dirty.
È sporco.
*eh SPOR-co.*

### It's overflowing.
Si è allagato.
*see eh a-la-GA-to.*

46

# Orientation

| **north** | nord | *nord* |
|-----------|------|--------|
| **south** | sud | *sood* |
| **east** | est | *est* |
| **west** | ovest | *o-VEST* |

**city map**
cartina della città
*kar-TEE-na de-la chee-TA*

**I'm lost.**
Mi sono perso/a.
*mee SO-no PER-so.*

**Can you tell me where the … is?**
Può dirmi dov'è …
*pwo DEER-mee do-VE …*

**Where is …**
Dov'è …
*do-VE …*

> **the tourist office?**
> l'ufficio turistico?
> *loo-FEE-cho too-REE-stee-co?*

> **the nearest restaurant?**
> il ristorante più vicino?
> *eel ree-sto-RAN-te pyoo vee-CHEE-no?*

> **the post office?**
> l'ufficio postale?
> *loo-FEE-cho po-STA-le?*

3

### the police station?
la stazione di polizia?
*la sta-TZYO-ne dee po-lee-TZEE-a?*

### the center of town?
il centro (città)?
*eel CHEN-tro (chee-TA)?*

---

### Can you tell me how to get there?
Può dirmi come arrivarci?
*pwo DEER-mee CO-me a-ree-VAR-chee?*

### Which way do I go?
Da che parte devo andare?
*da ke PAR-te DE-vo an-DA-re?*

---

### Turn ...
Gira ...
*JEE-ra ...*

#### left ...
a sinistra ...
*a see-NEE-stra ...*

#### right ...
a destra ...
*a DE-stra ...*

##### at the corner.
all'angolo.
*a-LAN-go-lo.*

##### at the next street.
alla prossima strada.
*a-la PRO-see-ma STRA-da.*

## Go straight ahead ...

Vai dritto ...

*vai DREE-to ...*

### down this street.

su questa strada.

*soo KWE-sta STRA-da.*

### through the intersection.

oltre l'incrocio.

*OL-tre leen-KRO-cho.*

---

## Am I going the right way?

Sto andando nella direzione giusta?

*sto an-DAN-do ne-la dee-re-TZYO-ne JOO-sta?*

## You're going the wrong way.

Stai andando nella direzione sbagliata.

*stai an-DAN-do ne-la dee-re-TZYO-ne zba-LYAT-a.*

## Do you have a map?

Hai una cartina?

*ai oo-na kar-TEE-na?*

---

## Can you recommend ...

Può raccomandarmi ...

*pwo ra-ko-man-DAR-mee ...*

### a place to eat?

un posto dove mangiare?

*oon PO-sto DO-ve man-JA-re?*

### a place to sleep?

un posto dove dormire?

*oon PO-sto DO-ve dor-MEE-re?*

### a trendy café?

un caffè alla moda?

*oon ka-FEH a-la MO-da?*

### a restaurant that's still open?
un ristorante ancora aperto?
*oon ree-sto-RAN-te an-KO-ra a-PER-to?*

### a bar?
un bar?
*oon bar?*

### a dance club / disco?
una discoteca?
*oo-na dee-sko-TE-ka?*

# Local Transportation

### Where's the nearest bus stop?
Dov'è la fermata dell'autobus più vicina?
*do-VE la fer-MA-ta de-lau-to-BOOS pyoo vee-CHEE-na?*

### Where can I catch the bus to [Piazza Navona]?
Dove ferma l'autobus per [Piazza Navona]?
*DO-ve FER-ma lau-to-BOOS per [PYA-tza na-VO-na]?*

### Do you stop at [the museum]?
Ferma al [museo]?
*FER-ma al [moo-ZE-o]?*

### Do you have a bus map?
Ha una cartina degli autobus?
*a oo-na kar-TEE-na de-lyee aw-to-BOOS?*

### What's the fare?
Quanto costa il biglietto?
*KWAN-to KO-sta eel bee-LYET-o?*

### Where's the nearest subway stop?
Dov'è la fermata della metro più vicina?
*do-VE la fer-MA-ta de-la ME-tro pyoo vee-CHEE-na?*

### I need ...
Vorrei ...
*vo-RE ...*

#### a ticket / token.
un biglietto / un gettone.
*oon bee-LYET-o / oon je-TO-ne.*

#### a day pass.
un giornaliero.
*oon jor-nal-YER-o.*

#### a weekly pass.
un settimanale.
*oon se-tee-ma-NA-le.*

#### a subway map.
una cartina della metro.
*oo-na kar-TEE-na de-la ME-tro.*

---

### transfer
biglietto cumulativo
*bee-LYET-o koo-moo-la-TEE-vo*

### the [red / A / 7] line
la linea [rossa / A / 7]
*la LEE-ne-a [RO-sa / a / SE-te]*

---

### Where do I get off?
Dove devo scendere?
*DO-ve DE-vo SHEN-de-re?*

#### At the first stop.
Alla prima fermata.
*A-la PREE-ma fer-MA-ta.*

#### At the second stop.
Alla seconda fermata.
*A-la se-KON-da fer-MA-ta.*

### Where can I catch a taxi?

Dove posso prendere un taxi?

*DO-ve PO-so PREN-de-re oon TA-ksee?*

### How much is a taxi to [the Colosseum]?

Quanto costa un taxi per andare [al Colosseo]?

*KWAN-to KO-sta oon TA-ksee per an-DA-re [al ko-lo-SE-o]?*

### What's the fare?

Quant'è?

*kwan-TE?*

### Please turn the meter on.

Per favore avvii il tassametro.

*per fa-VO-re a-VEE-ee eel ta-sa-ME-tro.*

### That's too much.

È troppo.

*eh TRO-po.*

# Wining and Dining

**4**

**I'm hungry.**
Ho fame.
*o FA-me.*

**I'm thirsty.**
Ho sete.
*o SE-te.*

**I'm starving.**
Sto morendo di fame.
*sto mo-REN-do dee FA-me.*

**I need to eat.**
Devo mangiare.
*DE-vo man-JA-re.*

**I could eat a horse.**
Potrei mangiare un bue.
*po-TRE man-JA-re oon BOO-e.*

**I need a drink.**
Ho bisogno di bere.
*o bee-ZO-nyo dee BE-re.*

**I need [several] drinks.**
Ho [molto] bisogno di bere.
*o [MOL-to] bee-ZO-nyo dee BE-re.*

# Meals

| breakfast | colazione | *ko-la-TZYO-ne* |
| --- | --- | --- |
| **lunch** | pranzo | *PRAN-zo* |
| **dinner** | cena | *CHE-na* |
| **snack** | merenda | *me-REN-da* |

# Courses

| salad | insalata | *een-sa-LA-ta* |
| --- | --- | --- |
| **appetizer** | antipasto | *an-tee-PA-sto* |
| **main course** | primo (piatto) | *PREE-mo (PYA-to)* |
| **side dish** | contorno | *kon-TOR-no* |
| **dessert** | dolce | *DOL-che* |

# Utensils

| fork | forchetta | *for-KE-ta* |
| --- | --- | --- |
| **knife** | coltello | *kol-TE-lo* |
| **spoon** | cucchiaio | *koo-KYAI-o* |
| **plate** | piatto | *PYA-to* |
| **bowl** | scodella | *sko-DE-la* |
| **cup** | tazza | *TA-tza* |
| **glass** | bicchiere | *bee-KYE-re* |

# Going Out to Eat

## Can you recommend a ...
Può raccomandarmi un ...
*pwo ra-ko-man-DAR-mee oon ...*

| | | |
|---|---|---|
| **restaurant?** | ristorante? | *ree-sto-RAN-te?* |
| **bar?** | bar? | *bar?* |
| **café?** | caffè? | *ka-FEH?* |

## Is it cheap?
È conveniente?
*eh kon-ven-YEN-te?*

## Is it nearby?
È vicino?
*eh vee-CHEE-no?*

## What kind of food do they serve?
Che tipo di cibo fanno?
*ke TEE-po dee CHEE-bo FA-no?*

## Do they have vegetarian food?
Hanno piatti vegetariani?
*A-no PYA-tee ve-je-tar-YA-nee?*

## Can they take a big group?
Prendono gruppi?
*PREN-do-no GROO-pee?*

## Will we need reservations?
Dobbiamo prenotare?
*do-BYA-mo pre-no-TA-re?*

## How late do they serve food?
Fino a che ora danno da mangiare?
*FEE-no a ke O-ra DA-no da man-JA-re?*

### We're in a hurry.
Abbiamo fretta.
*a-BYA-mo FRE-ta*

### We'd like a table for [four].
Vorremmo un tavolo per [quattro].
*vo-RE-mo oon TA-vo-lo per [KWA-tro].*

### How long is the wait?
Quanto c'è da aspettare?
*KWAN-to che da as-pe-TA-re?*

### We have a reservation.
Abbiamo una prenotazione.
*a-BYA-mo oo-na pre-no-ta-TZYO-ne.*

### The name is ...
A nome ...
*a NO-me ...*

### We'd like the [non]smoking section.
Vorremmo un tavolo nello spazio [non]fumatori.
*vo-RE-mo oon TA-vo-lo ne-lo SPA-tzyo [non]foo-ma-TO-ree.*

### My friends will be here ...
I miei amici saranno qui ...
*ee myay a-MEE-chee sa-RA-no kwee ...*

#### soon.
presto.
*PRE-sto.*

#### in [ten] minutes.
fra [dieci] minuti.
*fra [dee-E-chee] mee-NOO-tee.*

#### later.
più tardi.
*pyoo TAR-dee.*

4

### Where's the restroom?
Dove sono i servizi?
*DO-ve SO-no ee ser-VEE-tzee?*

### May I see a menu?
Posso vedere il menu?
*PO-so VE-de-re eel me-NOO?*

### What do you recommend?
Cosa mi suggerisce?
*KO-za mee soo-je-REE-she?*

### Do you have any specials?
C'è una specialità del giorno?
*che oo-na spe-cha-lee-TA del JOR-no?*

### Do you have a kids' menu?
Avete un menu per bambini?
*a-VE-te oon me-NOO per bam-BEE-nee?*

### I'm a vegetarian.
Sono vegetariano/a.
*SO-no ve-je-ta-RYA-no.*

### I'll have ...
Vorrei ...
*vo-RE ...*

### He / she will have ...
Lui / Lei prende ...
*LOO-ee / LE-ee PREN-de ...*

### I'll have what he / she's having.
Prendo quello che prende lui / lei.
*PREN-do KWE-lo ke PREN-de LOO-ee / LE-ee.*

### We'd like to split [an appetizer].
Vorremmo dividerci [un antipasto].
*vo-RE-mo dee-vee-DER-chee [oon an-tee-PA-sto].*

### Can you hold [the onions]?
Potrebbe non mettere [le cipolle]?
*po-TRE-be non ME-te-re [le chee-PO-le]?*

## Can I have [the sauce] on the side?
Posso avere [la salsa] a parte?
*PO-so a-VE-re [la SAL-sa] a PAR-te?*

---

## I'd like it ...
Lo / La vorrei ...
*lo / la vo-RE ...*

| | | |
|---|---|---|
| **rare.** | al sangue. | *al SAN-gwe.* |
| **medium.** | medio/a. | *ME-dee-o.* |
| **well done.** | ben cotto/a. | *ben KO-to.* |

---

## How is everything?
Tutto bene?
*TOO-to BE-ne?*

## Everything's great, thank you.
Va tutto benissimo, grazie.
*va TOO-to be-NEE-see-mo, GRA-tzee-e.*

---

## It's ...
È ...
*eh ...*

| | | |
|---|---|---|
| **delicious.** | squisito. | *skwee-ZEE-to.* |
| **bitter.** | amaro. | *a-MA-ro.* |
| **sour.** | acido. | *A-chee-do.* |
| **sweet.** | dolce. | *DOL-che.* |
| **hot / spicy.** | speziato. | *spe-TZYA-to.* |

## the best [artichoke] I've ever had.
il miglior [carciofo] che abbia mai mangiato.
*eel mee-LYOR [kar-CHO-fo] ke A-bee-a mai man-JA-to.*

### This is [a little] ...

È [un po'] ...
*eh [oon po] ...*

| | | |
|---|---|---|
| **cold.** | freddo. | FRE-do. |
| **undercooked.** | crudo. | KROO-do. |
| **overcooked.** | stracotto. | stra-KO-to. |
| **burnt.** | bruciato. | broo-CHA-to. |
| **too salty.** | troppo salato. | TRO-po sa-LA-to. |
| **not fresh.** | vecchio. | VE-kyo. |
| **rotten.** | marcio. | MAR-cho. |

### Can I have a new [napkin], please?
Posso avere un altro [tovagliolo], per favore?
*PO-so a-VE-re oon AL-tro [to-va-LYO-lo], per fa-VO-re?*

### This [fork] is dirty.
Questa [forchetta] è sporca.
*KWE-sta [for-KE-ta] eh SPOR-ka.*

### I'll have another.
Ne prendo un altro / un'altra.
*ne PREN-do oon AL-tro / oo-NAL-tra.*

### I'm full.
Sono sazio/a.
*SO-no SA-tzyo.*

### I'm stuffed.
Sono pieno/a.
*SO-no PYEN-o.*

### I'm still hungry.
Ho ancora fame.
*o an-KO-ra FA-me.*

### Can I take the rest to go?
Posso portarmi via il resto?
*PO-so por-TAR-mee VEE-a eel RE-sto?*

### The check, please.
Il conto, per favore.
*eel KON-to, per fa-VO-re.*

### Is tip / service included?
È incluso il servizio?
*eh een-KLOO-zo eel ser-VEE-tzyo?*

### I don't think the bill is right.
Non credo che il conto sia giusto.
*non KRE-do ke eel KON-to see-a JOO-sto.*

### Do you take credit cards?
Prendete la carta di credito?
*pren-DE-te la KAR-ta dee KRE-dee-to?*

### Can I get a receipt?
Posso avere una ricevuta?
*PO-so a-VE-re oo-na ree-che-VOO-ta?*

## Preparation

| | | |
|---|---|---|
| **raw** | crudo | *KROO-do* |
| **fresh** | fresco | *FRE-sco* |
| **baked** | al forno | *al FOR-no* |
| **fried** | fritto | *FREE-to* |
| **roasted** | arrosto | *a-RO-sto* |
| **grilled** | ai ferri | *a-ee FE-ree* |
| **sautéed** | saltato in padella | *sal-TA-to een pa-DE-la* |

| broiled | alla griglia / allo spiedo | *a-la GREE-lya /* *a-lo SPYED-o* |
| charred | alla brace | *a-la BRA-che* |

# Foods

| meat | carne | *KAR-ne* |
| --- | --- | --- |
| **beef** | manzo | *MAN-zo* |
| **ham** | prosciutto | *pro-SHOO-to* |
| **pork** | maiale | *mai-A-le* |
| **lamb** | agnello | *a-NYE-lo* |
| **poultry** | pollame | *po-LA-me* |
| **chicken** | pollo | *PO-lo* |
| **turkey** | tacchino | *ta-KEE-no* |

| fish | pesce | *PE-she* |
| --- | --- | --- |
| **salmon** | salmone | *sal-MO-ne* |
| **tuna** | tonno | *TO-no* |
| **bass** | branzino | *bran-TZEE-no* |
| **shrimp** | gamberetto | *gam-be-RE-to* |
| **squid** | calamaro | *ka-la-MA-ro* |

| fruit | frutta | *FROO-ta* |
| --- | --- | --- |
| **apple** | mela | *ME-la* |
| **orange** | arancia | *a-RAN-cha* |

| | | |
|---|---|---|
| **banana** | banana | *ba-NA-na* |
| **strawberry** | fragola | *FRA-go-la* |
| **cherry** | ciliegia | *chee-lee-E-ja* |
| **grapes** | uva | *OO-va* |

| | | |
|---|---|---|
| **vegetables / grains** | verdura / cereali | *ver-DOO-ra / che-re-A-lee* |
| **potato** | patata | *pa-TA-ta* |
| **tomato** | pomodoro | *po-mo-DO-ro* |
| **eggplant** | melanzana | *me-lan-ZA-na* |
| **cucumber** | cetriolo | *che-tree-O-lo* |
| **pepper** | peperone | *pe-pe-RO-ne* |
| **carrots** | carote | *ka-RO-te* |
| **onion** | cipolla | *chee-PO-la* |
| **garlic** | aglio | *A-lyo* |
| **mushroom** | fungo | *FOON-go* |
| **peas** | piselli | *pee-ZE-lee* |
| **corn** | mais | *mais* |
| **rice** | riso | *REE-zo* |
| **beans** | fagioli | *fa-JO-lee* |

| | | |
|---|---|---|
| **drinks** | bevande | *be-VAN-de* |
| **wine** | vino | *VEE-no* |
| **beer** | birra | *BEE-ra* |
| **liquor** | superalcolico | *soo-per-al-KO-lee-ko* |

4

WINING AND DINING

| | | |
|---|---|---|
| **soda / pop / Coke** | bibita / Coca | *BEE-bee-ta / KO-ka* |
| **water** | acqua | *A-kwa* |
| **still water** | naturale | *na-too-RA-le* |
| **carbonated** | gassata | *ga-SA-ta* |
| **coffee** | caffè | *ka-FEH* |
| **tea** | tè | *te* |
| **milk** | latte | *LA-te* |
| **juice** | succo | *SOO-ko* |

| | | |
|---|---|---|
| **spices** | spezie | *SPE-tzee-e* |
| **sugar** | zucchero | *TZOO-ke-ro* |
| **salt** | sale | *SA-le* |
| **pepper** | pepe | *PE-pe* |

| | | |
|---|---|---|
| **desserts** | dolci | *DOL-chee* |
| **cake** | torta | *TOR-ta* |
| **cookie** | biscotto | *bee-SKO-to* |
| **torte** | torta | *TOR-ta* |
| **cheese** | formaggio | *for-MA-jo* |

**I don't eat ...**
Non mangio ...
*non MAN-jo ...*

| | | |
|---|---|---|
| **red meat.** | carne rossa. | *KAR-ne RO-sa.* |
| **pork.** | maiale. | *mai-A-le.* |
| **fish.** | pesce. | *PE-she.* |

### I'm allergic ...
Sono allergico ...
*SO-no a-LER-jee-ko ...*

#### to nuts.
alle noci.
*A-le NO-chee.*

#### to chocolate.
al cioccolato.
*al cho-ko-LA-to.*

#### to dairy products.
ai latticini.
*ai la-tee-CHEE-nee.*

### I keep kosher.
Mangio kosher.
*MAN-jo KO-sher.*

### I'm vegan.
Sono vegan.
*SO-no VE-gan.*

### I'm Mormon.
Sono un mormone.
*SO-no oon mor-MO-ne.*

# 5 Grooming and Primping

---

## Clothes

**What are you wearing?**
Cosa indossi?
*KO-za   een-DO-see?*

---

**I'm wearing ...**
Indosso ...
*een-DO-so  ...*

> **a T-shirt.**
> una maglietta.
> *oo-na  ma-LYET-a.*
>
> **a [red] T-shirt.**
> una maglietta [rossa].
> *oo-na  ma-LYET-a  [ro-sa].*
>
> **a short-sleeve shirt.**
> una camicia a maniche corte.
> *oo-na  ka-MEE-cha  a  MA-nee-ke  KOR-te.*
>
> **a long-sleeve shirt.**
> una camicia a maniche lunghe.
> *oo-na  ka-MEE-cha  a  MA-nee-ke  LOON-ge.*

**a sweatshirt.**
una felpa.
*oo-na FEL-pa.*

**a sweater.**
un maglione.
*oon ma-LYON-e.*

**shorts.**
i pantaloncini.
*ee pan-ta-lon-CHEE-nee.*

**pants.**
i pantaloni.
*ee pan-ta-LO-nee.*

**jeans.**
i jeans.
*ee jeens.*

**a belt.**
una cintura.
*oo-na cheen-TOO-ra.*

**a skirt.**
una gonna.
*oo-na GO-na.*

**a dress.**
un vestito.
*oon ve-STEE-to.*

**a coat.**
un cappotto.
*oon ka-PO-to.*

**a jacket.**
una giacca.
*oo-na JA-ka.*

**a tank top.**
una canotta.
*oo-na ca-NO-ta.*

### a bra.
un reggiseno.
*oon re-jee-ZE-no.*

### a swimsuit.
un costume da bagno.
*oon ko-STOO-me da BA-nyo.*

### a bikini.
un due pezzi.
*oon DOO-e PE-tzee.*

### a hat.
un cappello.
*oon ka-PE-lo.*

### underwear.
la biancheria intima.
*la byan-ke-REE-a EEN-tee-ma.*

### tights.
i collant / le calze.
*ee ko-LANT / le KAL-tze.*

### nylons.
i collant / le calze di nailon.
*ee ko-LANT / le KAL-tze dee NAI-lon.*

### shoes.
le scarpe.
*le SKAR-pe.*

### sneakers.
le scarpe da ginnastica.
*le SKAR-pe da jee-NA-stee-ka.*

### sandals.
i sandali.
*ee SAN-da-lee.*

### boots.
gli stivali.
*lyee stee-VA-lee.*

### flats.
le scarpe basse.
*le SKAR-pe BA-se.*

### high heels.
i tacchi (alti).
*ee TA-kee (AL-tee).*

---

# Cleaning Up

### I need to ...
Devo / Ho bisogno di ...
*DE-vo / o bee-ZO-nyo dee ...*

#### take a shower.
fare una doccia.
*FA-re oo-na DO-cha.*

#### take a bath.
fare un bagno.
*FA-re oon BA-nyo.*

---

| | | |
|---|---|---|
| **towel** | asciugamano | *a-shoo-ga-MA-no* |
| **soap** | sapone | *sa-PO-ne* |
| **shampoo** | shampoo | *sham-POO* |
| **conditioner** | balsamo | *bal-SA-mo* |
| **lotion** | lozione | *lo-TZYO-ne* |
| **moisturizer** | idratante | *ee-dra-TAN-te* |
| **mirror** | specchio | *SPE-kyo* |

## The water is ...
L'acqua è ...
*LA-kwa  eh ...*

| **freezing.** | gelata. | *je-LA-ta.* |
| **too hot.** | troppo calda. | *TRO-po KAL-da.* |
| **just right.** | perfetta. | *per-FE-ta.* |
| **brown.** | marrone. | *ma-RO-ne.* |

## I need to ...
Devo ...
*DE-vo ...*

### brush my teeth.
lavarmi i denti.
*la-VAR-mee  ee  DEN-tee.*

### floss.
passarmi il filo interdentale.
*pa-SAR-mee  eel  FEE-lo  een-ter-den-TA-le.*

### do my hair.
sistemarmi i capelli.
*see-ste-MAR-mee  ee  ka-PE-lee.*

### brush my hair.
spazzolarmi i capelli.
*spa-tzo-LAR-mee  ee  ka-PE-lee.*

### comb my hair.
pettinarmi (i capelli).
*pe-tee-NAR-mee  (ee  ka-PE-lee).*

### dry my hair.
asciugarmi i capelli.
*a-shoo-GAR-mee  ee  ka-PE-lee.*

### put on makeup.
truccarmi.
*troo-KAR-mee.*

### clean out my earwax.
togliermi il cerume.
*to-LYER-mee eel che-ROO-me.*

---

## Have you seen ...
Hai visto ...
*ai VEE-sto ...*

### my toothbrush?
il mio spazzolino da denti?
*eel mee-o spa-tzo-LEE-no da DEN-tee?*

### the hair dryer?
l'asciugacapelli?
*la-shoo-ga-ka-PE-lee?*

# Getting Ready

## I don't have anything to wear.
Non ho niente da mettermi.
*non o NYEN-te da ME-ter-mee.*

## I'm ready!
Sono pronto/a!
*SO-no PRON-to!*

## I need more time.
Mi serve più tempo.
*mee SER-ve pyoo TEM-po.*

## [Five] more minutes.
Ancora [cinque] minuti.
*an-KO-ra [CHEEN-kwe] mee-NOO-tee.*

### I'll meet you ...
Ci vediamo ...
*chee ve-DYA-mo ...*

#### outside.
fuori.
*FWO-ree.*

#### in the lobby.
nell'atrio.
*ne-LA-tree-o.*

#### at the restaurant.
al ristorante.
*al ree-sto-RAN-te.*

### You look great.
Stai benissimo.
*stai be-NEE-see-mo.*

### You've aged well.
Sei invecchiato/a bene.
*se een-ve-KYA-to BE-ne.*

### I look terrible!
Sto malissimo!
*sto ma-LEE-see-mo!*

### Is this outfit appropriate?
Vado bene vestito/a così?
*VA-do BE-ne ve-STEE-to ko-ZEE?*

## Do you have ...
Hai ...
*ai ...*

### money?
dei soldi?
*de-ee SOL-dee?*

### your ID?
la tua carta d'identità?
*la too-a KAR-ta dee-den-tee-TA?*

---

## I can't find my ...
Non riesco a trovare ...
*non RYES-ko a tro-VA-re ...*

| | | |
|---|---|---|
| **purse.** | la borsa. | *la BOR-sa.* |
| **wallet.** | il portafoglio. | *eel por-ta-FO-lyo.* |
| **keys.** | le chiavi. | *le KYA-vee.* |

---

## Are you bringing [a bag]?
Ti porti [la borsa]?
*tee POR-tee [la BOR-sa]?*

# 6 Going Out

## Making Plans

**What are you up to tonight?**
Che hai voglia di fare stasera?
*ke ai VO-lya dee FA-re sta-SE-ra?*

**You feel like doing something?**
Hai voglia di fare qualcosa?
*ai VO-lya dee FA-re kwal-KO-za?*

> **Yeah, I'd love to.**
> Sì, mi piacerebbe.
> *see, mee pya-che-RE-be.*
>
> **Maybe.**
> Forse.
> *FOR-se.*
>
> **Not sure yet.**
> Non lo so ancora.
> *non lo so an-KO-ra.*
>
> **No, I can't, sorry.**
> No, non posso, scusa.
> *no, non PO-so, SKOO-za.*
>
> **No, I'm tired.**
> No, sono stanco/a.
> *no, SO-no STAN-ko.*

### I'm staying in.
Sto in casa.
*sto een KA-za.*

### Call me if it seems fun.
Chiamami se è divertente.
*KYA-ma-mee se e dee-ver-TEN-te.*

---

### What do you feel like doing?
Che ti va di fare?
*ke tee va dee FA-re?*

### Did you eat yet?
Hai già mangiato?
*ai ja man-JA-to?*

### Have you talked to [John]?
Hai parlato con [John]?
*ai par-LA-to kon [john]?*

---

### I'm in the mood for ...
Ho voglia di ...
*o VO-lya dee ...*

### We could ...
Potremmo ...
*po-TRE-mo ...*

#### go to a movie.
andare a vedere un film.
*an-DA-re a VE-de-re oon film.*

#### go to a show.
andare a uno spettacolo.
*an-DA-re a oo-no spe-TA-ko-lo.*

#### go out to dinner.
andare a cena fuori.
*an-DA-re a CHE-na FWO-ree.*

### get drinks.
bere qualcosa.
*BE-re kwal-CO-za.*

### go on a bender.
ubriacarci.
*oo-brya-KAR-chee.*

### hang out in my room.
stare in camera mia.
*STA-re een KA-me-ra MEE-a.*

### Where should we go?
Dove possiamo andare?
*DO-ve po-SYA-mo an-DA-re?*

### I love that place.
Adoro quel posto.
*a-DO-ro kwel PO-sto.*

### I hate that place.
Detesto quel posto.
*de-TE-sto kwel PO-sto.*

### I've never been there.
Non ci sono mai stato/a.
*non chee SO-no mai STA-to.*

### I heard it gets a good crowd.
Ho sentito che c'è bella gente.
*o sen-TEE-to ke che BE-la JEN-te.*

### Is it close by?
È vicino?
*eh vee-CHEE-no?*

### Is it far?
È lontano?
*eh lon-TA-no?*

### What time does it open?
A che ora apre?
*a ke O-ra A-pre?*

### What time does it close?
A che ora chiude?
*a ke O-ra KYOO-de?*

---

### What time do you want to meet?
A che ora vuoi che ci vediamo?
*a ke O-ra vwoy ke chee ve-DYA-mo?*

### How long do you need to get ready?
Di quanto hai bisogno per prepararti?
*dee KWAN-to ai bee-ZO-nyo per pre-pa-RAR-tee?*

### I'm free at ...
Sono libero/a alle ...
*SO-no LEE-be-ro A-le ...*

### Okay, I'll call you at ...
Bene, ti chiamo alle ...
*BE-ne, tee KYA-mo A-le ...*

### What are you going to wear?
Cosa ti metti?
*KO-za tee ME-tee?*

### What should I wear?
Cosa mi metto?
*KO-za mee ME-to?*

### Do I have to dress formally?
Devo vestirmi elegante?
*DE-vo ve-STEER-mee e-le-GAN-te?*

### Do we need a reservation?
Dobbiamo prenotare?
*do-BYA-mo pre-no-TA-re?*

GOING OUT

### Is there dancing?

Si balla?

*see BA-la?*

### Do they ask for ID?

Chiedono la carta d'identità?

*KYE-do-no la KAR-ta dee-den-tee-TA?*

### What time does the [show] start?

A che ora inizia [lo spettacolo]?

*a ke O-ra ee-NEE-tzya [lo spe-TA-ko-lo]?*

### How late will you be out?

Fino a che ora stai fuori?

*FEE-no a ke O-ra stai FWO-ree?*

### I have something to do in the morning.

Ho da fare domattina.

*o da FA-re do-ma-TEE-na.*

### Let's make it an early night.

Rientriamo presto.

*ree-en-TRYA-mo PRE-sto.*

### Let's go wild!

Scateniamoci!

*ska-te-NYA-mo-chee!*

### Where do you want to meet?

Dove vuoi che ci vediamo?

*DO-ve vwoy ke chee ve-DYA-mo?*

### Let's meet at ...

Vediamoci da ...

*ve-DYA-mo-chee da ...*

### What street is it on?

Su che strada è?

*soo ke STRA-da eh?*

### I'll meet you there.
Ci vediamo là.
*chee ve-DYA-mo la.*

### Call me if you get lost.
Chiamami se ti perdi.
*KYA-ma-mee se tee PER-dee.*

### Where are you?
Dove sei?
*DO-ve se?*

### I'm running late.
Sono in ritardo.
*SO-no een ree-TAR-do.*

### I'll be there in [ten] minutes.
Arrivo tra [dieci] minuti.
*a-REE-vo tra [dee-E-chee] mee-NOO-tee.*

# At the Bar

### I love this place!
Adoro questo posto!
*a-DO-ro KWE-sto PO-sto!*

### Let's stay a little longer.
Restiamo ancora un po'.
*re-STYA-mo an-KO-ra oon po.*

### Do you see a table anywhere?
Vedi un tavolo da qualche parte?
*VE-dee oon TA-vo-lo da KWAL-ke PAR-te?*

### I'll be by the bar.
Sono al bar.
*SO-no al bar.*

### This place sucks.
Questo posto fa schifo.
*KWE-sto PO-sto fa SKEE-fo.*

### Let's go somewhere else.
Andiamo da qualche altra parte.
*an-DYA-mo da KWAL-ke AL-tra PAR-te.*

### Let's go back to that other place.
Torniamo in quell'altro posto.
*tor-NYA-mo een kwe-LAL-tro PO-sto.*

### Let's go home.
Andiamo a casa.
*an-DYA-mo a KA-za.*

---

### I'm tired.
Sono stanco/a.
*SO-no STAN-ko.*

### I'm not tired yet.
Non sono ancora stanco/a.
*non SO-no an-KO-ra STAN-ko.*

### I'm just getting started.
Ho appena cominciato.
*o a-PE-na ko-meen-CHA-to.*

---

### I'm out of cash.
Non ho contanti.
*non o kon-TAN-tee.*

### This place is too expensive.
Questo posto costa troppo.
*KWE-sto PO-sto KO-sta TRO-po.*

### Can you loan me some money?
Puoi prestarmi dei soldi?
*pwoy pre-STAR-mee de-ee SOL-dee?*

### Is there an ATM around here?
C'è un bancomat qua vicino?
*che oon BAN-ko-mat kwa vee-CHEE-no?*

### Do you have a light?

Hai da accendere?
*ai da a-CHEN-de-re?*

### Do you have a cigarette?

Hai una sigaretta?
*ai oo-na see-ga-RE-ta?*

### Do you want a drink?

Vuoi da bere?
*vwoy da BE-re?*

### What do you like to drink?

Cosa bevi?
*KO-za BE-vee?*

**6**

---

## Pickup Lines

**Come here often?**
Vieni qui spesso?
*VYEN-ee kwee SPE-so?*

**Is everyone from [Italy] as pretty as you?**
[Le italiane] sono tutte belle come te?
*[le ee-tal-YA-ne] so-no TOO-te BE-le KO-me te?*

**Is everyone from [Italy] as handsome as you?**
[Gli italiani] sono tutti belli come te?
*[lyee ee-tal-YA-nee] SO-no TOO-tee BE-lee KO-me te?*

**Are you sure you're not from heaven?**
**Because you look like an angel.**
Sei sicuro/a di non venire dal Paradiso?
Perché sembri un angelo.
*se see-KOO-ro dee non ve-NEE-re dal pa-ra-DEE-zo?*
*per-KE SEM-bree oon AN-je-lo.*

**Don't fall in love with me. I'm bad news.**
Non innamorarti di me. Sono pericoloso/a.
*non ee-na-mo-RAR-tee dee me. SO-no pe-ree-ko-LO-zo.*

**Let's get to know each other.**
Conosciamoci meglio.
*ko-no-SHA-mo-chee ME-lyo.*

### Tell me about yourself.
Dimmi di te.
*DEE-mee dee te.*

### What do you do?
Che fai?
*ke fai?*

### What music / films / books do you like?
Che musica / film / libri ti piace / piacciono?
*ke MOO-zee-ka / feelm / LEE-bree tee PYA-che / PYA-cho-no?*

### Are you from here?
Sei di qua?
*se dee kwa?*

### Where do you live?
Dove vivi?
*DO-ve VEE-vee?*

| **Cool!** | Forte! | *FOR-te!* |
| **Great!** | Grande! | *GRAN-de!* |
| **Fascinating!** | Affascinante! | *a-fa-shee-NAN-te!* |
| **Me too!** | Anch'io! | *an-KEE-o!* |

### You're ...
Sei ...
*se ...*

| **pretty.** | carina. | *ka-REE-na.* |
| **beautiful.** | bella. | *BE-la.* |
| **handsome.** | bello. | *BE-lo.* |
| **stunning.** | meraviglioso/a. | *me-ra-vee-LYO-zo.* |

## You'e one of the most beautiful women / men I've ever seen.
Sei una delle donne più belle / uno degli uomini più belli che abbia mai visto.

*se oo-na de-le DO-ne pyoo BE-le / oo-no de-lyee WO-mee-nee pyoo BE-lee ke a-BEE-a mai VEE-sto.*

## I like you.
Mi piaci.

*mee PYA-chee.*

## You seem nice.
Sembri simpatico/a.

*SEM-bree seem-PA-tee-ko.*

---

## You have ...
Hai ...

*ai ...*

### such beautiful eyes.
dei bellissimi occhi.

*de-ee be-LEE-see-mee O-kee.*

### such beautiful hair.
dei bellissimi capelli.

*de-ee be-LEE-see-mee ka-PE-lee.*

### such beautiful hands.
delle bellissime mani.

*de-le be-LEE-see-me MA-nee.*

---

## I'm interested in you.
Mi interessi.

*mee een-te-RE-see.*

## Do you have a [boyfriend / girlfriend]?
Hai [un ragazzo / una ragazza]?

*ai [oon ra-GA-tzo / oo-na ra-GA-tza]?*

### My [boyfriend / girlfriend] is out of town (this weekend).

[Il mio ragazzo / La mia ragazza] è fuori città (questo fine settimana).

*[eel mee-o ra-GA-tzo / la mee-a ra-GA-tza] e FWO-ree chee-TA (KWE-sto FEE-ne se-tee-MA-na).*

# Rejection

### I'm here with my [boyfriend / girlfriend].

Sono qui con [il mio ragazzo / la mia ragazza].
*SO-no kwee con [eel mee-o ra-GA-tzo / la mee-a ra-GA-tza].*

### I'm sorry, but I'm not interested.

Mi dispiace, non mi interessa.
*mee dee-SPYA-che, non mee een-te-RE-sa.*

### You're just not my type.

Non sei il mio tipo.
*non se eel mee-o TEE-po.*

### Please leave me alone.

Lasciami stare, per favore.
*LA-sha-mee STA-re, per fa-VO-re.*

### Get away from me!

Vattene!
*va-TE-ne!*

### Security!

Sicurezza!
*see-koo-RE-tza!*

### Are you gay?

Sei gay?
*se gey?*

### I'm gay.

Sono gay.
*SO-no gey.*

### I'm straight.
Sono etero(sessuale).
*SO-no E-te-ro(se-SWA-le).*

### It's a pity you aren't gay.
Peccato che tu non sia gay.
*pe-KA-to ke too non SEE-a gey.*

### I'm bisexual.
Sono bisessuale.
*SO-no bee-se-SWA-le.*

### I'm transgendered.
Sono trans.
*SO-no trans.*

### I used to be a [man / woman].
Prima ero [un uomo / una donna].
*PREE-ma E-ro oon [WO-mo / oo-na DO-na].*

# Love at First Sight

### Can I stay over?
Posso dormire qui?
*PO-so dor-MEE-re kwee?*

### I want you to stay over.
Voglio che dormi qui.
*VO-lyo ke DOR-mee kwee.*

### Let's spend the night together.
Passiamo la notte insieme.
*pa-SYA-mo la NO-te een-SYE-me.*

### We can watch the sunrise.
Possiamo guardare l'alba.
*po-SYA-mo gwar-da-re LAL-ba.*

### Kiss me.
Baciami.
*BA-cha-mee.*

### It's better if you go home.
È meglio che vai a casa.
*e ME-lyo ke vai a KA-za.*

### I'd better go.
Meglio che vada.
*ME-lyo ke VA-da.*

### I think we should stop.
Penso che dovremmo fermarci.
*PEN-so ke dov-RE-mo fer-MAR-chee.*

### I have to go home now.
Devo andare a casa adesso.
*DE-vo an-DA-re a KA-za a-DE-so.*

### I had a great time.
Sono stato/a benissimo.
*SO-no STA-to be-NEE-see-mo.*

### Thanks for a lovely evening.
Grazie per la bella serata.
*GRA-tzee-e per la BE-la se-RA-ta.*

### Here's my number.
Questo è il mio numero.
*KWE-sto e eel mee-o NOO-me-ro.*

### I'm here for [three] more days.
Mi fermo altri [tre] giorni.
*mee FER-mo AL-tree [tre] JOR-nee.*

---

### Can we meet tomorrow?
Ci vediamo domani?
*chee ve-DYA-mo do-MA-nee?*

### Can I see you again?
Posso rivederti?
*PO-so ree-ve-DER-tee?*

### When can I see you?
Quando posso rivederti?
*KWAN-do PO-so ree-ve-DER-tee?*

### Where do you want to meet?
Dove vuoi che ci vediamo?
*DO-ve vwoy ke chee ve-DYA-mo?*

---

### Are you seeing someone else?
Vedi qualcun altro?
*VE-dee kwal-KOON AL-tro?*

### He / she's just a friend.
È solo un amico / un'amica.
*eh SO-lo oon a-MEE-ko / oo-na-MEE-ka.*

### I think we should just be friends.
Penso che dovremmo essere solo amici.
*PEN-so ke dov-RE-mo E-se-re SO-lo a-MEE-chee.*

---

### I love you!
Ti amo!
*tee A-mo!*

### I'm in love with you!
Sono innamorato/a di te!
*SO-no ee-na-mo-RA-to dee te!*

### You should come visit me.
Dovresti venire a trovarmi.
*dov-RE-stee ve-NEE-re a tro-VAR-mee.*

### Let's become pen pals.
Scriviamoci.
*skree-VYA-mo-chee.*

### What's your email?
Qual è la tua email?
*kwal eh la too-a ee-MEIL?*

### I promise to write you.

Prometto di scriverti.

*pro-ME-to dee skree-VER-tee.*

### I'll never forget you.

Non ti dimenticherò mai.

*non tee dee-men-tee-ke-RO mai.*

### Our time together has meant a lot to me.

Questo periodo ha significato molto per me.

*KWE-sto pe-REE-o-do ha see-nyee-fee-KA-to MOL-to per me.*

### What was your name again?

Come hai detto che ti chiami?

*KO-me ai DE-to ke tee KYA-mee?*

# 8 Seeing the Sights

## Sights

**I'd like to see ...**
Vorrei vedere ...
*vo-RE VE-de-re ...*

> **the museum.**
> il museo.
> *eel moo-ZE-o.*

> **the art gallery.**
> la galleria d'arte.
> *la ga-le-REE-a DAR-te.*

> **the palace.**
> il palazzo.
> *eel pa-LA-tzo.*

> **the castle.**
> il castello.
> *eel ka-STE-lo.*

> **the church.**
> la chiesa.
> *la KYE-za.*

> **the cathedral.**
> la cattedrale.
> *la ka-te-DRA-le.*

**the park.**
il parco.
*eel PAR-ko.*

**the gardens.**
i giardini.
*ee jar-DEE-nee.*

**the zoo.**
lo zoo.
*lo tzoo.*

**the ruins.**
le rovine.
*le ro-VEE-ne.*

**the cemetery.**
il cimitero.
*eel chee-mee-TE-ro.*

**some art.**
un po' di arte.
*oon po dee AR-te.*

**some historical sites.**
dei siti storici.
*de-ee SEE-tee STO-ree-chee.*

**the downtown area.**
il centro.
*eel CHEN-tro.*

**the historic district.**
il centro storico.
*eel CHEN-tro STO-ree-ko.*

**the shopping district.**
la zona commerciale.
*la TZO-na ko-mer-CHA-le.*

**the red-light district.**
la zona a luci rosse.
*la TZO-na a LOO-chee RO-se.*

### Do you have any ...
Hai qualche ...
*ai KWAL-ke ...*

**brochures?** depliant? *de-plee-ANT?*

**maps?** cartina? *kar-TEE-na?*

**suggestions?** suggerimento? *soo-je-ree-MEN-to?*

### I'd like to go on a ...
Vorrei fare un ...
*vo-RE FA-re oon ...*

**walking tour.**
giro a piedi.
*JEE-ro a PYED-ee.*

**guided tour.**
giro turistico.
*JEE-ro too-REE-stee-ko.*

**bus tour.**
giro in autobus.
*JEE-ro een ow-to-BOOS.*

**boat tour.**
giro in nave.
*JEE-ro een NA-ve.*

### Where can I hire a guide / interpreter?
Dove posso trovare una guida / un interprete?
*DO-ve PO-so tro-VA-re oo-na GWEE-da / oon een-TER-pre-te?*

### What's the nicest part of the city?
Qual è la parte più carina della città?
*kwal eh la PAR-te pyoo ka-REE-na de-la chee-TA?*

### What's your favorite neighborhood?
Qual è il tuo quartiere preferito?
*kwal eh eel too-o kwar-TYE-re pre-fe-REE-to?*

### Is this area safe?

Quest'area è sicura?

*kwe-STA-re-a eh see-KOO-ra?*

### What should I see if I'm here only one day?

Cosa dovrei vedere se mi fermo solo un giorno?

*KO-za dov-RE VE-de-re se mee FER-mo SO-lo oon JOR-no?*

### Where's the best place to watch the sunrise / sunset?

Qual è il posto migliore dove vedere l'alba / il tramonto?

*kwal e eel PO-sto mee-LYO-re DO-ve VE-de-re LAL-ba / eel tra-MON-to?*

## Calling Ahead

### Where does the tour start?

Dove inizia il giro?

*DO-ve ee-NEE-tzya eel JEE-ro?*

### What time does it start?

A che ora inizia?

*a ke O-ra ee-NEE-tzya?*

### How long is it?

Quanto dura?

*KWAN-to DOO-ra?*

### What stops does it make?

Che fermate fa?

*ke fer-MA-te fa?*

### Do I have to reserve a spot?

Devo prenotare un posto?

*DE-vo pre-no-TA-re oon PO-sto?*

### What hours are you open?

A che ora siete aperti?

*a ke O-ra SYET-e a-PER-tee?*

### When do you close?
Quando chiudete?
*KWAN-do kyoo-DE-te?*

### What do you charge for admission?
Quanto costa l'ingresso?
*KWAN-to CO-sta leen-GRE-so?*

### Is there a student discount?
Fate uno sconto studenti?
*FA-te oo-no SKON-to stoo-DEN-tee?*

### Is there a group discount?
Fate uno sconto comitive?
*FA-te oo-no SKON-to ko-mee-TEE-ve?*

# Cultural Stuff

### Let's go to ...
Andiamo ...
*an-DYA-mo ...*

#### the theater.
a teatro.
*a te-A-tro.*

#### the movies.
al cinema.
*al CHEE-ne-ma.*

#### a show.
a vedere uno spettacolo.
*a VE-de-re oo-no spe-TA-ko-lo.*

#### a concert.
a un concerto.
*a oon kon-CHER-to.*

#### the opera.
all'opera.
*a-LO-pe-ra.*

### an exhibit.
a una mostra.
*a  oo-na  MO-stra.*

### a soccer game.
a vedere una partita di calcio.
*a  VE-de-re  oo-na  par-TEE-ta  dee  KAL-cho.*

### a bullfight.
a vedere una corrida.
*a  VE-de-re  oo-na  ko-REE-da.*

~~~~~~~~~~~~~~~~~~~

### Where's the movie playing?
In che cinema danno il film?
*een  ke  CHEE-ne-ma  DA-no  eel  feelm?*

### What time does the show start?
A che ora inizia lo spettacolo?
*a  ke  O-ra  ee-NEE-tzya  lo  spe-TA-ko-lo?*

### How much are the tickets?
Quanto costano i biglietti?
*KWAN-to  KO-sta-no  ee  bee-LYET-ee?*

### Do you have any tickets left for tonight?
Avete ancora biglietti per stasera?
*a-VE-te  an-KO-ra  bee-LYET-ee  per  sta-SE-ra?*

### Is tonight's performance sold out?
Lo spettacolo di stasera è esaurito?
*lo  spe-TA-ko-lo  de  sta-SE-ra  eh  e-zow-REE-to?*

# Going Broke

## Money

### I want to go shopping.
Voglio andare a far compere.
*VO-lyo an-DA-re a far KOM-pe-re.*

### Where can I change money?
Dove posso cambiare dei soldi?
*DO-ve PO-so kam-BYA-re de-ee SOL-dee?*

### What's the exchange rate?
Quant'è il cambio?
*kwan-TE eel KAM-byo?*

### Is there a(n) ... around here?
C'è un / una ... da queste parti?
*che oon / oo-na ... da KWE-ste PAR-tee?*

> **bank**
> banca
> *BAN-ka*
>
> **ATM**
> bancomat
> *BAN-ko-mat*
>
> **store**
> negozio
> *ne-GO-tzyo*

### market
mercato
*mer-KA-to*

### mall
centro commerciale
*CHEN-tro   ko-mer-CHA-le*

### department store
grande magazzino
*GRAN-de   ma-ga-TZEE-no*

### grocery store
alimentari
*a-lee-men-TA-ree*

### supermarket
supermercato
*soo-per-mer-KA-to*

### drugstore / pharmacy
farmacia
*far-ma-CHEE-a*

### bookstore
libreria
*lee-bre-REE-a*

**souvenir shop**
negozio di souvenir
*ne-GO-tzyo dee soo-ve-NEER*

**casino**
casinò
*ka-zee-NO*

# At the Store

**I need to buy ...**
Devo comprare ...
*DE-vo kom-PRA-re ...*

**Do you sell ...**
Vendete ...
*ven-DE-te ...*

**I'm looking for ...**
Sto cercando ...
*sto cher-KAN-do ...*

| | | |
|---|---|---|
| **clothes.** | vestiti. | *ve-STEE-tee.* |
| **souvenirs.** | souvenir. | *soo-ve-NEER.* |
| **postcards.** | cartoline. | *kar-to-LEE-ne.* |
| **stamps.** | francobolli. | *fran-ko-BO-lee.* |
| **a map.** | una cartina. | *oo-na kar-TEE-na.* |
| **a guidebook.** | una guida. | *oo-na GWEE-da.* |
| **an umbrella.** | un ombrello. | *oon om-BRE-lo.* |

**I need a gift for ...**
Vorrei un regalo per ...
*vo-RE oon re-GA-lo per ...*

### my friend.
il mio amico / la mia amica.
*eel mee-o a-MEE-ko / la mee-a a-MEE-ka.*

### my parents.
i miei genitori.
*ee myay je-nee-TO-ree.*

### my brother / sister.
mio fratello / mia sorella.
*mee-o fra-TE-lo / mee-a so-RE-la.*

### my boyfriend / girlfriend.
il mio ragazzo / la mia ragazza.
*eel mee-o ra-GA-tzo / la mee-a ra-GA-tza.*

### Can you suggest anything?
Ha qualche suggerimento?
*a KWAL-ke soo-je-ree-MEN-to?*

### I'm just browsing, thanks.
Sto solo guardando, grazie.
*sto SO-lo gwar-DAN-do, GRA-tzee-e*

---

### That's ...
È ...
*eh ...*

| | | |
|---|---|---|
| **nice.** | carino/a. | *ka-REE-no.* |
| **perfect.** | perfetto/a. | *per-FE-to.* |
| **beautiful.** | bello/a. | *BE-lo.* |
| **lovely.** | grazioso/a. | *gra-TZYO-zo.* |
| **ugly.** | brutto/a. | *BROO-to.* |
| **hideous.** | orrendo/a. | *o-REN-do.* |
| **divine.** | divino/a. | *dee-VEE-no.* |

### I like it.
Mi piace.
*mee PYA-che.*

### I don't like it.
Non mi piace.
*non me PYA-che.*

### Is it handmade?
È fatto a mano?
*eh FA-to a MA-no?*

### Can I try it on?
Posso provarlo/la?
*PO-so pro-VAR-lo?*

### How does this look?
Come mi sta?
*KO-me mee sta?*

### It doesn't look good on me.
Non mi sta bene.
*non mee sta BE-ne.*

### It doesn't fit me.
Non mi sta.
*non mee sta.*

---

### Do you have something ...
Ha qualcosa ...
*a kwal-KO-za ...*

#### cheaper?
meno caro?
*ME-no KA-ro?*

#### fancier?
più originale?
*pyoo o-ree-jee-NA-le?*

### in a bigger size?
in una taglia più grande?
*een oo-na TA-lya pyoo GRAN-de?*

### in a smaller size?
in una taglia più piccola?
*een oo-na TA-lya pyoo PEE-ko-la?*

### in a different color?
in un altro colore?
*een oon AL-tro ko-LO-re?*

### Is anything on sale?
C'è qualcosa in saldo?
*che kwal-KO-za een SAL-do?*

# Haggling

### How much does this cost?
Quanto costa questo?
*KWAN-to ko-sta KWE-sto?*

### That's ...
Quello è ...
*KWE-lo eh ...*

> #### a bargain.
> un affare.
> *oon a-FA-re.*
>
> #### too expensive.
> troppo caro.
> *TRO-po KA-ro.*
>
> #### a complete ripoff.
> un vero furto.
> *oon ve-ro FOOR-to.*

## Can I get a lower price?
Mi fa un po' meno?
*mee fa oon po ME-no?*

## I'll offer you half that.
Le do la metà.
*le do la me-TA.*

# Paying

## I have cash.
Ho dei contanti.
*o de-ee kon-TAN-tee.*

## I don't have change.
Non ho spiccioli.
*non o SPEE-cho-lee.*

## Do you take ...
Prendete ...
*pren-DE-te ...*

### credit cards?
carte di credito?
*KAR-te dee KRE-dee-to?*

### checks?
assegni?
*a-SE-nyee?*

### traveler's checks?
traveler's checks?
*TRA-ve-lers cheks?*

### Can you wrap it for me?
Me lo impacchetta?
*me lo eem-pa-KE-ta?*

### Can I get it shipped home?
Me lo può spedire a casa?
*me lo pwo spe-DEE-re a KA-za?*

### Can I get it delivered?
Me lo può far consegnare a casa?
*me lo pwo far kon-se-NYA-re a KA-za?*

### The address is ...
L'indirizzo è ...
*leen-dee-REE-tzo eh ...*

### I need to return this.
Devo restituire questo.
*DE-vo re-stee-TWEE-re KWE-sto.*

# 10 Killing Time

## Doing Nothing

**What do you feel like doing?**
Cosa hai voglia di fare?
*KO-za ai VO-lya dee FA-re?*

**Do you play ...**
Giochi a ...
*JO-kee a ...*

| | | |
|---|---|---|
| **cards?** | carte? | *KAR-te?* |
| **checkers?** | dama? | *DA-ma?* |
| **chess?** | scacchi? | *ska-kee?* |

**I win.**
Ho vinto.
*o VEEN-to.*

**You lose.**
Hai perso.
*ai PER-so.*

**,ain.**
ncora.
*KO-ra.*

**1.**
te.
*TEN-te.*

### You're learning fast.
Impari velocemente.
*eem-PA-ree ve-lo-che-MEN-te.*

### You suck at this.
Sei una schiappa.
*se oo-na SKYA-pa.*

### I just want to ...
Voglio solo ...
*VO-lyo SO-lo ...*

#### stay in.
stare in casa.
*STA-re een KA-za.*

#### relax.
rilassarmi.
*ree-la-SAR-mee.*

#### sit at a café.
sedermi a un caffè.
*se-DER-mee a oon ka-FEH.*

#### go read somewhere.
andare a leggere da qualche parte.
*an-DA-re a LE-je-re da KWAL-ke PAR-te.*

#### go for a walk.
andare a fare una passeggiata.
*an-DA-re a FA-re oo-na pa-se-JA-ta.*

# The Beach

**Let's go to the beach.**
Andiamo in spiaggia.
*an-DYA-mo een SPYA-ja.*

---

**Where can I buy ...**
Dove posso comprare ...
*DO-ve PO-so kom-PRA-re ...*

### a beach towel?
un telo da mare?
*oon TE-lo da MA-re?*

### a beach chair?
una sedia sdraio?
*oo-na SE-dya ZDRAI-o?*

### a beach umbrella?
un ombrellone?
*oon om-bre-LO-ne?*

### a swimsuit?
un costume da bagno?
*oon ko-STOO-me da BA-nyo?*

### flip-flops?
dei sandali infradito?
*de-ee SAN-da-lee een-fra-DEE-to?*

### sunscreen?
della crema solare?
*de-la KRE-ma so-LA-re?*

### trashy novels?
dei romanzi spazzatura?
*de-ee ro-MAN-tzee spa-tza-TOO-ra?*

### I need to put on sunscreen.
Devo mettermi la crema.
*DE-vo ME-ter-mee la KRE-ma.*

### Am I getting burned?
Mi sto scottando?
*mee sto sko-TAN-do?*

### You're getting burned.
Ti stai scottando.
*tee stai sko-TAN-do.*

---

### You're ...
Sei ...
*se ...*

> #### tan.
> abbronzato/a.
> *a-bron-TZA-to.*
>
> #### sunburned.
> scottato/a.
> *sco-TA-to.*
>
> #### really white.
> bianchissimo/a.
> *byan-KEE-see-mo.*

---

### Can you swim here?
Si può fare il bagno qui?
*see pwo FA-re eel BA-nyo kwee?*

### Is there a lifeguard?
C'è il bagnino?
*che eel ba-NYEE-no?*

### How deep is the water?
Quant'è profonda l'acqua?
*kwan-TE pro-FON-da LA-kwa?*

## Let's go swimming.
Andiamo a fare il bagno.
*an-DYA-mo a FA-re eel BA-nyo.*

## Come on in.
Entra.
*EN-tra.*

~~~~~~~~~~~~~~~~~

## The water's ...
L'acqua è ...
*LA-kwa eh ...*

### great.
fantastica.
*fan-TA-stee-ka.*

### warm.
calda.
*KAL-da.*

### cold.
fredda.
*FRE-da.*

### shallow.
bassa.
*BA-sa.*

### deep.
profonda.
*pro-FON-da.*

### rough.
burrascosa.
*boo-ra-SKO-za.*

### full of jellyfish.
piena di meduse.
*PYEN-a dee me-DOO-ze.*

### teeming with sharks.
brulicante di squali.
*broo-lee-KAN-te dee SKWA-lee.*

### Don't swim out too far.
Non nuotare troppo lontano.
*non nwo-TA-re TRO-po lon-TA-no.*

### Where's the nude beach?
Dov'è la spiaggia nudista?
*do-VE la SPYA-ja noo-DEE-sta?*

### Let's go ...
Andiamo a ...
*an-DYA-mo a ...*

##### snorkeling.
fare snorkeling.
*FA-re SNOR-ke-leeng.*

##### scuba diving.
fare immersioni sub.
*FA-re ee-mer-SYO-nee soob.*

##### fishing.
pescare.
*pe-SKA-re.*

##### rent a boat.
noleggiare una barca.
*no-le-JA-re oo-na BAR-ka.*

##### rent a Jet Ski.
noleggiare un Jet Ski.
*no-le-JA-re oon jet skee.*

### Where is the ...
Dov'è ...
*do-VE ...*

##### dock?
il molo?
*eel MO-lo?*

### dive shop?
il negozio di attrezzatura sub?
*eel ne-GO-tzyo dee a-tre-tza-TOO-ra soob?*

### marina?
il porticciolo?
*eel por-tee-CHO-lo?*

~~~~~~~~~~

### Can I rent ... here?
Posso noleggiare ... qui?
*PO-so no-le-JA-re ... kwee?*

#### equipment
l'attrezzatura
*la-tre-tza-TOO-ra*

#### a wetsuit
una tuta subacquea
*oo-na TOO-ta soo-BA-kwe-a*

#### a mask
una maschera
*oo-na MAS-ke-ra*

# Sports

### Do you like to ...
Ti piace ...
*tee PYA-che ...*

#### play sports?
fare sport?
*FA-re sport?*

#### play soccer?
giocare a calcio?
*jo-KA-re a KAL-cho?*

#### play tennis?
giocare a tennis?
*jo-KA-re a TE-nees?*

### play basketball?
giocare a pallacanestro?
*jo-KA-re a pa-la-ka-NE-stro?*

### play golf?
giocare a golf?
*jo-KA-re a golf?*

### swim?
nuotare?
*nwo-TA-re?*

### bike?
andare in bici?
*an-DA-re een BEE-chee?*

### jog?
correre?
*ko-RE-re?*

### ski?
sciare?
*SHYA-re?*

### do yoga?
fare yoga?
*FA-re YO-ga?*

### go sailing?
andare in barca a vela?
*an-DA-re een BAR-ka a VE-la?*

### go skating?
andare a pattinare?
*an-DA-re a pa-tee-NA-re?*

### go diving?
andare a fare immersioni?
*an-DA-re a FA-re ee-mer-SYO-nee?*

### go horseback riding?
andare a cavallo?
*an-DA-re a ka-VA-lo?*

### I'm not very good at this.
Non sono molto bravo/a.
*non SO-no MOL-to BRA-vo.*

### You're great at this!
Sei bravissimo/a!
*se bra-VEE-see-mo!*

### Let's race to the end.
Facciamo una corsa fino in fondo.
*Fa-CHYA-mo oo-na KOR-sa FEE-no een FON-do.*

### This is fun.
È divertente.
*eh dee-ver-TEN-te.*

### I'm tired.
Sono stanco/a.
*SO-no STAN-ko.*

### I'd like to go to the gym.
Vorrei andare in palestra.
*vo-RE an-DA-re een pa-LE-stra.*

### Is there a gym around here?
C'è una palestra da queste parti?
*che oo-na pa-LE-stra da KWE-ste PAR-tee?*

### Do you have ...
Avete ...
*a-VE-te ...*

> #### free weights?
> i pesi?
> *ee PE-zee?*
>
> #### cardio equipment?
> attrezzatura cardio?
> *a-tre-tza-TOO-ra KAR-dyo?*

### a pool?
una piscina?
*oo-na pee-SHEE-na?*

### a sauna?
una sauna?
*oo-na sa-OO-na?*

### a treadmill?
il tapis roulant?
*eel ta-PEE roo-LAN?*

### stair machines?
delle stair machine?
*de-le STA-er ma-SHEEN?*

### personal trainers?
dei personal trainer?
*de-ee PER-so-nal TRA-ee-ner?*

## Do you offer ...
Avete ...
*A-VE-te ...*

### aerobics?
corsi di aerobica?
*KOR-see dee ae-RO-bee-ka?*

### classes?
corsi?
*KOR-see?*

## How much is a ...
Quanto costa un ...
*KWAN-to KO-sta oon ...*

### day pass?
ingresso giornaliero?
*een-GRE-so jor-nal-YER-o?*

**week pass?**
abbonamento settimanale?
*a-bo-na-MEN-to se-tee-ma-NA-le?*

**month pass?**
abbonamento mensile?
*a-bo-na-MEN-to men-SEE-le?*

**year pass?**
abbonamento annuale?
*a-bo-na-MEN-to a-NWA-le?*

# Renting a Car

**Where can I rent a car?**
Dove posso noleggiare un'auto?
*DO-ve PO-so no-le-JA-re oon-OW-to?*

**What's the daily rate?**
Quanto costa al giorno?
*KWAN-to KO-sta al JOR-no?*

**How much is insurance?**
Quanto costa l'assicurazione?
*KWAN-to KO-sta la-see-koo-ra-TZYO-ne?*

**Here's my license.**
Ecco la mia patente.
*E-ko la mee-a pa-TEN-te.*

**There's a dent in it.**
È ammaccata.
*eh a-ma-KA-ta.*

**The paint is scratched.**
La vernice è graffiata.
*la ver-NEE-che eh gra-FYA-ta.*

**Where can I buy gas?**
Dove posso fare benzina?
*DO-ve PO-so FA-re ben-TZEE-na?*

### road signs
i segnali stradali
*ee se-NYA-lee stra-DA-lee*

| | | |
|---|---|---|
| **stop** | stop | *stop* |
| **yield** | precedenza | *pre-che-DEN-za* |
| **one way** | senso unico | *SEN-so OO-nee-ko* |
| **detour** | deviazione | *de-vee-a-TZYO-ne* |
| **toll** | pedaggio | *pe-DA-jo* |
| **parking** | parcheggio | *par-KE-jo* |

# The Outdoors

### Do you know good places for ...
Conosci un buon posto dove ...
*ko-NO-shee oon bwon PO-sto DO-ve ...*

#### hiking?
fare hiking?
*FA-re AI-keeng?*

#### mountain biking?
andare in mountain bike?
*an-DA-re een MOWN-tan baik?*

#### rock climbing?
fare arrampicate?
*FA-re a-ram-pee-KA-te?*

#### seeing animals?
vedere gli animali?
*VE-de-re lyee a-nee-MA-lee?*

### I need to rent ...
Devo noleggiare ...
*DE-vo  no-le-JA-re ...*

#### a tent.
una tenda.
*oo-na TEN-da.*

#### a sleeping bag.
un sacco a pelo.
*oon SA-ko a PE-lo.*

#### hiking boots.
degli scarponcini.
*de-lyee skar-pon-CHEE-nee.*

#### a flashlight.
una pila.
*oo-na PEE-la.*

#### a backpack.
uno zaino.
*oo-no TZAI-no.*

#### a mountain bike.
una mountain bike.
*oo-na MOWN-tan baik.*

#### a canteen.
una borraccia.
*oo-na bo-RA-cha.*

---

### Do you have trail maps?
Avete degli itinerari delle escursioni?
*a-VE-te de-lyee ee-tee-ne-RA-re de-le es-koor-ZYO-nee?*

## Is this trail ...

Questo itinerario è ...
*KWE-sto ee-tee-ne-RA-ryo e ...*

| **hard?** | difficile? | *dee-FEE-chee-le?* |
|---|---|---|
| **easy?** | facile? | *FA-chee-le?* |
| **hilly?** | collinoso? | *ko-lee-NO-zo?* |
| **flat?** | piatto? | *PYA-to?* |
| **well-marked?** | ben segnalato? | *ben se-nya-LA-to?* |
| **scenic?** | pittoresco? | *pee-to-RE-sko?* |
| **long?** | lungo? | *LOON-go?* |
| **short?** | corto? | *KOR-to?* |
| **grueling?** | estenuante? | *e-sten-oo-AN-te?* |

## Is the water safe to drink?

Si può bere quest'acqua?
*see pwo BE-re kwe-STA-kwa?*

## What's the weather supposed to be like ...

Quali sono le previsioni per ...
*KWA-lee SO-no le pre-vee-ZYO-nee per ...*

### today?
oggi?
*O-jee?*

### tomorrow?
domani?
*do-MA-nee?*

### this week?
questa settimana?
*KWE-sta se-tee-MA-na?*

### this weekend?
questo fine settimana?
*KWE-sto FEE-ne se-tee-MA-na?*

### Is it supposed to ...
Prevedono ...
*pre-VE-do-no ...*

#### rain?
pioggia?
*PYO-ja?*

#### snow?
neve?
*NE-ve?*

#### storm?
temporali?
*tem-po-RA-lee?*

#### get cold?
freddo?
*FRE-do?*

#### get hot?
caldo?
*KAL-do?*

#### get below freezing?
gelate?
*je-LA-te?*

KILLING TIME

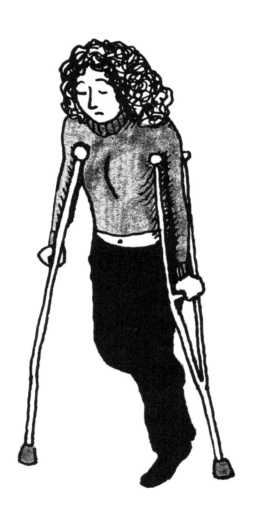

## Ailments

**I don't feel well.**
Non mi sento bene.
*non mee SEN-to BE-ne.*

**My ... hurts. / I have a ...ache.**
Ho mal di ...
*o mal dee...*

| | | |
|---|---|---|
| **head** | testa. | *TE-sta.* |
| **stomach** | stomaco. | *STO-ma-ko.* |
| **throat** | gola. | *GO-la.* |
| **ear** | orecchio. | *o-RE-kyo.* |
| **tooth** | dente. | *DEN-te.* |
| **neck** | collo. | *KO-lo.* |
| **back** | schiena. | *SKYEN-a.* |
| **feet** | piedi. | *PYED-ee.* |

**That hurts.**
Fa male.
*fa MA-le.*

**I have pain here.**
Mi fa male qui.
*mee fa MA-le kwee.*

## I feel …
Mi sento …
*mee SEN-to* …

| | | |
|---|---|---|
| **better.** | meglio. | *ME-lyo.* |
| **worse.** | peggio. | *PE-jo.* |
| **dizzy.** | stordito. | *stor-DEE-to.* |
| **faint.** | debole. | *DE-bo-le.* |
| **weird.** | strano. | *STRA-no.* |

## I have …
Ho …
*o* …

| | | |
|---|---|---|
| **a cold.** | il raffreddore. | *eel ra-fre-DO-re.* |
| **a fever.** | la febbre. | *la FE-bre.* |
| **chills.** | i brividi. | *ee BREE-vee-dee.* |
| **nausea.** | la nausea. | *la NOW-ze-a.* |
| **diarrhea.** | la diarrea. | *la dee-a-RE-a.* |

## I threw up.
Ho vomitato.
*o vo-mee-TA-to.*

## I think I broke …
Penso di essermi rotto/a …
*PEN-so de E-ser-mee RO-to* …

### my arm.
un braccio.
*oon BRA-cho.*

**my finger.**
un dito.
*oon DEE-to.*

**my wrist.**
un polso.
*oon POL-so.*

**my toe.**
un dito del piede.
*oon DEE-to del PYED-e.*

**my ankle.**
una caviglia.
*oo-na ka-VEE-lya.*

**my foot.**
un piede.
*oon PYED-e.*

**my leg.**
una gamba.
*oo-na GAM-ba.*

**my rib.**
una costola.
*oo-na KO-sto-la.*

**my collarbone.**
la clavicola.
*la kla-VEE-ko-la.*

---

**Is it broken?**
È rotto/a?
*eh RO-to?*

**Is it infected?**
Ha un'infezione?
*eh oo-neen-fe-TZYO-ne?*

# Medicine and Prescriptions

**I ran out of medicine.**
Ho finito le medicine.
*o fee-NEE-to le me-dee-CHEE-ne.*

**I need a refill.**
Devo ricomprarle.
*DE-vo ree-kom-PRAR-le.*

**I need a new prescription.**
Mi serve un'altra ricetta.
*mee SER-ve oo-NAL-tra ree-CHE-ta.*

**11**

STAYING HEALTHY

**I'm allergic ...**
Sono allergico/a ...
*SO-no a-LER-jee-ko ...*

> **to ibuprofen.**
> all'ibuprofene.
> *a-lai-boo-PRO-fe-ne.*

> **to penicillin.**
> alla penicillina.
> *A-la pe-nee-chee-LEE-na.*

> **to aspirin.**
> all'aspirina.
> *a-la-spee-REE-na.*

> **to bee stings.**
> alle punture delle api.
> *A-le poon-TOO-re de-le A-pee.*

> **to nuts.**
> alle noci.
> *A-le NO-chee.*

**I'm diabetic.**
Sono diabetico/a.
*SO-no dee-a-BE-tee-ko.*

**I have asthma.**
Ho l'asma.
*o LAS-ma.*

# Toiletries

**I need to buy ...**
Devo comprare ...
*DE-vo kom-PRA-re ...*

>   **Band-Aids.**
>   dei cerotti.
>   *de-ee che-RO-tee.*
>
>   **sunscreen.**
>   della crema solare.
>   *de-la KRE-ma so-LA-re.*
>
>   **toothpaste.**
>   del dentifricio.
>   *del den-tee-FREE-cho.*
>
>   **a toothbrush.**
>   uno spazzolino.
>   *oo-no spa-tzo-LEE-no.*

>   **a razor.**
>   un rasoio.
>   *oon ra-ZOY-o.*
>
>   **shaving cream.**
>   della schiuma da barba.
>   *de-la SKYOO-ma da BAR-ba.*
>
>   **makeup.**
>   dei cosmetici.
>   *de-ee kos-ME-tee-chee.*

**tampons.**
degli assorbenti interni.
*de-lyee a-sor-BEN-tee een-TER-nee.*

**a hairbrush.**
una spazzola.
*oo-na SPA-tzo-la.*

**new glasses.**
degli occhiali nuovi.
*de-lyee o-KYAL-ee NWO-vee.*

**new contact lenses.**
delle lenti a contatto nuove.
*de-le LEN-tee a con-TA-to NWO-ve.*

**contact lens solution.**
della soluzione per lenti a contatto.
*de-la so-loo-TZYO-ne per LEN-tee a con-TA-to.*

# Emergencies

**Help!**
Aiuto!
*ay-OO-to!*

**Go away!**
Va' via!
*va VEE-a!*

**Leave me alone!**
Lasciami stare!
*LA-sha-mee STA-re!*

**Thief!**
Ladro!
*LA-dro!*

**It's an emergency.**
È un'emergenza.
*e oo-ne-mer-JEN-za.*

### Call the police!
Chiama la polizia!
*KYA-ma la pol-ee-TZEE-a!*

### Call an ambulance!
Chiama un'ambulanza!
*KYA-ma oo-nam-boo-LAN-za!*

### Call a doctor!
Chiama un dottore!
*KYA-ma oon do-TO-re!*

### I need help.
Ho bisogno di aiuto.
*o bee-ZO-nyo dee ay-OO-to.*

### I'm lost.
Mi sono perso/a.
*me SO-no PER-so.*

# Crime

### I was mugged.
Mi hanno rapinato.
*me A-no ra-pee-NA-to.*

### I was assaulted.
Mi hanno aggredito.
*mee A-no a-gre-DEE-to.*

### I lost ... / Someone stole ...
Ho perso ... / Mi hanno rubato ...
*o PER-so ... / mee A-no roo-BA-to ...*

#### my passport.
il passaporto.
*eel pa-sa-POR-to.*

**my wallet.**
il portafoglio.
*eel por-ta-FO-lyo.*

**my purse.**
la borsa.
*la BOR-sa.*

**my camera.**
la macchina fotografica.
*la MA-kee-na fo-to-GRA-fee-ka.*

**my cell phone.**
il cellulare.
*eel che-loo-LA-re.*

**my laptop.**
il computer portatile.
*eel kom-PYOO-ter por-TA-tee-le.*

**my glasses.**
gli occhiali.
*lyee o-KYAL-ee.*

**my luggage.**
il bagaglio.
*eel ba-GA-lyo.*

**my backpack.**
lo zaino.
*lo TZAI-no.*

**my (tour) group.**
il mio gruppo (del tour).
*eel mee-o GROO-po (del toor).*

**my mind.**
la testa.
*la TES-ta.*

**my virginity.**
la verginità.
*la ver-jee-nee-TA.*

# Grammar in Five Minutes

## Pronouns

Here are some of the most important words you'll need for Italian: the **personal pronouns**.

| SINGULAR | | PLURAL | |
|---|---|---|---|
| **I** | io | **we** | noi |
| **you** (informal) | tu | **you all** (informal) | voi |
| **you** (formal) | Lei | **you all** (formal) | Loro |
| **he** | lui | **they** | loro |
| **she** | lei | | |

## Politeness and Formality

Italian speakers distinguish between **formal and informal forms of "you"** when addressing different people. To be on the safe side, use tu only when speaking with close friends or with children. Use Lei when addressing anyone else, especially if they're older than you.

## Gender

One thing about Italian that always throws English speakers for a loop: **all Italian nouns have a gender.** Often, there's no logic behind this system: what makes a book (un libro) a "he" and a car (una macchina) a "she" is anyone's guess.

Not only are nouns gendered, but any **adjectives** that describe nouns are gendered as well. An old book is un libro vecchio, but an old car is una macchina vecchia. You'll still get your point across even if you make mistakes with this, so don't worry about it too much.

## Adjectives After Nouns

As you saw with un libro vecchio, **adjectives in Italian come after the noun.** This is the opposite of English—we say "the old book," not "the book old." Although there are a few oddball adjectives in Italian that often come before the noun, this noun-then-adjective rule is nearly universal.

## Five Essential Verbs in the Present Tense

All Italian verbs are **conjugated**—modified slightly in form to reflect who's performing the action of the verb. English verbs are conjugated too—the verb "to be" changes to "I am," "you are," "he is," etc.—but our system is much less complex. Here are five essential Italian verbs, conjugated fully in the present tense. If you can memorize these, you'll be at a huge advantage.

### to be – essere

| SINGULAR | | PLURAL | |
|---|---|---|---|
| io | sono | noi | siamo |
| tu | sei | voi | siete |
| lui/lei/Lei | è | loro/Loro | sono |

### to have – avere

| | | | |
|---|---|---|---|
| io | ho | noi | abbiamo |
| tu | hai | voi | avete |
| lui/lei/Lei | ha | loro/Loro | hanno |

### to do, to make – fare

| | | | |
|---|---|---|---|
| io | faccio | noi | facciamo |
| tu | fai | voi | fate |
| lui/lei/Lei | fa | loro/Loro | fanno |

### to want – volere

| | | | |
|---|---|---|---|
| io | voglio | noi | vogliamo |
| tu | vuoi | voi | volete |
| lui/lei/Lei | vuole | loro/Loro | vogliono |

### to go – andare

| | | | |
|---|---|---|---|
| io | vado | noi | andiamo |
| tu | vai | voi | andate |
| lui/lei/Lei | va | loro/Loro | vanno |

# Acknowledgments

Special thanks to our writer, Chiara Marchelli, who contributed enormously both to this project and to the other Italian titles in our study cards and SparkCharts series.

Super special thanks to our illustrator, Frank Webster, who took time out from traveling the globe in his private dirigible, *The Princess Calliope*, to supply the wonderful illustrations on the cover and throughout this book.